Yoga Studio Marketing

MATHIEU
VAN STEENBERGE

Mathieu Van Steenberge
Yoga Studio Marketing

© 2018, Mathieu Van Steenberge

Self-published
mathieuvansteenberge@gmail.com

Contents

Acknowledgments

First, my sincere and special thanks go out to Bart De Bondt. As Country Manager at a now publicly listed Internet company, I faced great challenges with my team. The pressure to achieve results, accomplish growth and to perform is very high here and gathering a winning team acquires a lot of effort of all team members involved. Bart and I initially crossed paths to ensure an even better functioning of my team and to provide insight into ourselves and the other team members. What started as team coaching, soon evolved into a painful confrontation with myself. Bart knew how to make me confront myself like no one else and forced me to really be honest with myself, my ambitions in this life and the people around me. Bart has succeeded to break through my outer appearance and allowed the voice coming from my heart to speak louder. Thank you, Bart, for stirring up the fire within me and to provide me with courage and determination. Meeting you has been the first step in exploring my true purpose of life, to live more with less and finally become the man behind the mask.

Special thanks to Benny Demeulenaere as well. What seemed like an incidental meeting at first has proven not so incidental today. If it weren't for the short run-in at the "random" Italian restaurant in the heart of Amsterdam, I would have never started yoga.

Thank you to all my (yoga) teachers and especially Dolly Voeten for continuously inspiring me, giving me opportunities and for reading this book first and sharing your feedback with me.

Many thanks to the curious souls that I have met during my trainings and retreats. I feel blessed to have met so many warm, loving people. They all, each in their own way, play a part in making this world a better and more respectful place.

Thanks Doris Diederichsen for the unique cover photo (taken at 'Monthana Encantada', Brazil).

An extra special thanks goes to Chantal Elzinga and Marije Evertse. I originally wrote this book in Dutch and distributed it for free. When people started to ask for an English version, I reached out to all the people that have downloaded this book and that's how I met Chantal and Marije. It's thanks to these wonderful ladies who spend hours and hours translating, that I can offer this book in English, reaching and supporting more "yogi-entrepreneurs".

Finally, I would also like to thank family, friends and acquaintances that I have met on my journey and that have given me the strength to continue the path that I have chosen. From the deepest of my heart, I thank you!

Peace & Love,
Mathieu

Introduction

As a welcomed and needed guide for the 'yogi-entrepreneur,' Mathieu offers this gift of his years of experience in the business world to Yoga studio owners as an informative tool to build a successful business while maintaining a high level of integrity and connection to the essence of Yoga. While the various aspects of Yoga offer practitioners insight to the nature of the Self, Mathieu's insights offer practical tools, tips and functional information to the nature of running a Yoga business. As a former Yoga studio owner, current traveling teacher and independent businessman I know the challenges of running a successful business in today's competitive Yoga climate. Yes, it is an unfortunate truth that there is competition in a subject that strives to cultivate equanimity and this is where a business model that aims to support the overall expansion of Yoga must be applied. Rather than looking at 'yours' and 'mine,' Yoga businesses can follow a greater vision of creating programs, courses, trainings and events that feed the totality of humanity which in turn supports other teachers and studios. When we all are successful at finding, supporting and keeping students then the success multiplies. This book is such a tool as it is written with a business exterior and a Yogi interior.

Having taught at over 110 Yoga studios on 5 continents, I have experienced many ways of running a 'yoga business' and I am happy to see such a beautiful guide being offered to build the bridge between the many varied paths of practicing Yoga and the ability to be financially and socially successful with a studio. Also having a business degree, I know that when the 'heart' is removed from making a profit that it is not a sustainable business on very important levels. Although fairly "new" to the path of Yoga, Mathieu captures the essence of deeper teachings and the authenticity of an experienced Yogi in this business focused guide showing great steps to make positive shifts in the world by building successful Yoga studios that thrive in their respective communities.

David Lurey
Founder & Director of Find Balance Yoga
www.findbalance.net

'Yoga. It just isn't for me'. Those were my thoughts after my dear friend (who happens to be a yoga teacher) showed me how to do sun salutations. Luckily, that same friend later invited me to spend a couple of days at a yoga festival on one of the Dutch islands. I fell in love with yoga right then and there (the second time's a charm ;-)) I vividly remember thinking that the world would be a better place if every single person were doing yoga.

I have been practicing yoga ever since, whether it is on or off the mat. Not only that, I became a Hatha yoga and a children's yoga teacher. I feel it is my purpose to help make yoga available to everyone, regardless of their limitations. That is why I feel blessed to also be teaching Yoga for the Special Child® This method has deepened my own yoga practice and enabled me to connect with the person behind the special needs.

By writing this book (and having it translated), Mathieu has definitely contributed to making my heartfelt wish (of yoga being made available to everyone) come true. By buying this book, you will have done the same. My gratitude is endless.

Chantal Elzinga
Translator & Yogini

At 17 years of age, I fell in love with the French city of Lyon. 8 years later I decided to follow my heart and move to France. During my first period in this new city, I quickly found a few good yoga studios and met some very talented and kind teachers.

I am blessed to be a part of this yoga-community today, and to have recently started my own Yoga Café in Lyon, based at the restaurant of my partner Nicolas.
This new chapter in my life combines the three things that I adore most in life: yoga, food and of course... love.

Taking risks and following your heart can be a good thing, but it is wise to have a solid foundation and the knowledge to back up your projects.
Mathieu's book offered real help in this undertaking and has proven to be extremely relevant. If you are at all interested in working on opening your own studio, this book filled with information will help you during your journey.

Marije Evertse
Translator & Yogini

Preface

Through the conversations with the local and foreign yoga studio owners, it became clear to me that many yoga studios are founded from a dream to work with yoga full-time. The reality shows that running a yoga studio means more than organizing and teaching yoga classes. Continuously attracting and nurturing students are one of the biggest challenges that yoga studio owners are confronted with.

From my passion for marketing and entrepreneurship, I randomly shared marketing tips here and there with yoga studio owners I met on my yoga-path. Soon it became clear that I want to share my knowledge with as many (future) yoga studio owners as possible. On the one hand because I have great admiration for people that are passionately chasing their dreams, and on the other hand because I have been bitten by the yoga-bug which makes me want to introduce as many people as possible to the physical, mental and spiritual benefits that yoga has to offer, together with you (future) yoga studio owners. The more yoga studios I can support in their growth, the more people we can reach together and allow them to become acquainted with the joys that yoga has to offer.

Are you being confronted with the challenges of opening a yoga studio? Or in becoming an established certified yoga teachers? Or attracting students in a competitive neighborhood? Or getting your yoga studio financially healthy? With this book in hand I can assure you that you are no longer alone. Many successful yoga teachers and yoga studio owners have had to figure out – through trial and error – how to make a profession out of their passion. Why should you have to go through the same ordeal, if we can combine this knowledge and spread it so that everybody can start their entrepreneurial adventure well prepared? Have fun reading and learning!

"Feel like I'm making progress on getting to know my clients better, and I love the idea of a free class on your birthday, but still so much to do. You've motivated me to look into online business management software as I think this will simplify my life and also help me track better what's going on in my business. I want to work smarter, not harder -- and get back to doing what I love, which is teaching!!!"

Courtenay Willis
www.treeoflifeyoga.be

Important:
To the reader of this book

Since my budget is limited, I unfortunately haven't found anyone willing to proofread the entire book to check for grammatical mistakes. People make mistakes. I am a person. Therefore, I make mistakes. Have you come across a typo or an awkward phrase? Contact me as soon as you can and the readers and I will be forever grateful.

Obviously, everyone contributing to the finalization of this book will receive an honorable mention and extra karma points.

Finally, I would like to emphasize that this book has been written to inspire you and to provide pointers on how to launch and expand your yoga studio in a healthy way. It's not because you're not doing something or because you decide to do it in a different way that you're not doing it "right". There is not one specific recipe for success; my most important advice would be to critically consider everything (**including this book**) and to follow the path the heart leads you to while using your common (business & people) sense. Stay true to yourself and work authentically (keeping the yama's and niyama's in mind) is the first and most important lesson if you want to successfully apply marketing. I do not have a patent on the truth and there are undoubtedly valuable insights, experiences, marketing techniques and –ideas that I haven't covered in this book. Do you have additions, constructive feedback or a "golden tip" that you would like to share with the readers and myself? Contact me and I would love to hear you story, feedback and ideas. *Sharing is caring!*

Warm salutations,
Mathieu

Feel free to connect with me:
www.facebook.com/mathieuvansteenberge
www.instagram.com/mathieuvansteenberge

Chapter 1

The start

Alright; you have decided to run a yoga studio: Yes! Congratulations! Good for you! You have worked so hard to realize your dream. Finally you dare to shake up your comfortable life and take the leap. Maybe you even quit a well-paying job to get started with this adventure; because you've been dreaming about yoga, freedom, "doing your own thing" every night and day. Done with the rut of a fixed job you were doing since you needed to pay the rent every month. Welcome to the authentic "me" who can finally do what he/she was made for. There are few certainties, but it is beyond doubt that yoga is your life. YOU breathe YOGA and would like to share this with the entire world; or at least starting off with your local community.

As an ambitious and undertaking yogi, you have had years of teaching experience, maybe even one or several teacher trainings and many workshops. There you were, in your living room, with your first student. Your own home studio was born, and soon after you received a second, third and even a fourth student, until suddenly your room became too small and you had to move to the local fitness studio or parish where the memory of coffee circles, solemn communions and scouting parties is never far. Your students –hypnotized by the vibration of your OM and obviously impressed by your teaching techniques by now – followed you full of admiration and with pleasure. On top of that you got more and more students. The satisfaction you got gave you even more inspiration and energy. In your head a seed was planted with the idea to open up your own yoga studio at some point. Years spent deepening the knowledge with regards to asanas, pranayama, mantras and the eightfold path of Patanjali. Finally you gathered all your courage, energy, knowledge and savings for this final moment with the ultimate goal to open up your own yoga studio.

With this book held in your hand, the seed that was planted in your mind so many years ago is no longer a seed but reality. A reality that was first shaped in your head the first couple of years and that now exists in the real world. Your seed has become a beautiful tree. This tree is inhabited by dozens of chirping and fluttering birds. But there are other trees in this forest, many other trees. The leafage of the other trees may block the sun to leave your tree in the shadows. This great oak, that has been dominating the forest for years, will not automatically make space for a young little tree that has recently started rooting in the soft soil of the forest. Your tree will have to grow, and maybe get replanted to a place where the sun can shine on the green leafs. The birds fly from one tree to another. Sometimes they will hang around your tree for a bit, only to fly off to the fruits of the tree next to yours. Soon it becomes clear that a tree – to become a large and healthy tree – needs more than just a seed and a nutritious soil. It is not surprising that you sometimes can't seem to see the forest for the trees. Something has to happen, or even change, but you just don't know what and who can help you with this. Besides, there is such a large offer and so many opportunities; this too makes it difficult to see the so-called forest for the trees. With this book I would like to offer fierce and hardworking *tree planters* the insights to supply your tree with a fixed place in the forest so that it can grow out to become a true attraction for playing, singing and fluttering birds. Or just for the birds that are passing through and want to take a rest on one of your firm branches before they continue their trail.

The metaphor of the forest properly summarizes the

challenges that I have heard of during my conversations with entrepreneurial yogis. Do you remember what expectations you had when you decided to open a yoga studio? Do these correspond to the reality? Can you finally do you own thing? Do you only need to hold responsibility to yourself? Do you now know for what and whom you work? Do you finally have the freedom you where yearning for when you went through life with a paid job and yoga was merely a hobby? You probably found out very quickly that teaching a yoga class is something completely different than running your own studio. Though you were busy with yoga almost all the time when you were teaching, as a business owner you get confronted with a 1001 different – but not inconsiderable – matters that have little to do with yoga. Have you ever asked yourself what takes up most of your time today and does this correspond with what you HAVE to spend most time on *and* what you WANT to spend most time on? Your to-do list keeps growing, your work-life balance is disordered and everything that is coming at you seems like a priority. Feelings of guilt that you're not doing everything 'perfectly' arise. Moreover, you struggle with having to (continuously) attract students as thereasons for your existence. This is a challenge for many talented entrepreneurial yogis for which unfortunately, because of the daily chores of running a yoga studio, there is little time. If your yoga studio is the heart then your students are the blood. Without blood the heart cannot pump and without blood the heart cannot get oxygen and will die. Summed up, your yoga studio needs students.

Questions such as how to attract new students, how activate these students to return *and* how to earn a bit of extra money in addition to the yoga classes to be able to finally have a little left over for yourself – after paying all your bills –, will be addressed with practical examples in this book.

This book is written in such a way that you won't have to read each chapter one after the other. You could – depending on your personal knowledge and needs – decide to start with chapter 7 and end with chapter 4.

Chapter 2

Everybody marketeer!

With this book I mostly want to offer practical tips and marketing insights that you can get started with immediately. If you are looking for a theoretical reference on marketing I will have to disappoint you. Are you looking to learn more about marketing in all its facets, however, I can recommend you the following reading material:

- "Purple Cow: Transform Your Business by Being Remarkable"
  - By Seth Godin

- "Contagious: Why Things Catch On"
  - By Jonah Berger

- "Marketing Fundamentals, An International Perspective"
  - By Bronis Verhage

- "Marketing Management"
  - By Philip Kotler & Kevin Lane Keller

Before taking you through practical and elaborated marketing techniques, I would like to take a moment to reflect on several definitions of marketing. Not that one of the definitions below is *the* definition, but because you will quickly determine that you – although not always consciously – are often working on marketing in your yoga studio, more than you would think. Everybody marketer!

"Marketing is the process of communicating the value of a product or service to customers, for the purpose of selling that product or service. From a societal point of view, marketing is the link between a society's material requirements and its economic patterns of response. Marketing satisfies these needs and wants through exchange processes and building long term relationships. Marketing can be looked at as an organizational function and a set of processes for creating, delivering and communicating value to customers, and managing customer relationships in ways that also benefit the organization and its shareholders. Marketing is the science of choosing target markets through market analysis and market segmentation, as well as understanding consumer buying behavior and providing superior customer value." – **Wikipedia**

The thing I like in this definition is that the word "customers" is mentioned no less than four times. The link to long-term relations with these customers also shows that marketing revolves around building relationships and that a relation demands an (time) investment and is not a one-time activity.

"Marketing is the activity, set of institutions, and processes for creating, communicating, delivering, and exchanging offerings that have value for customers, clients, partners, and society at large." – **American Marketing Association (AMA)**

The AMA tried – after debating for years – to give a comprehensive but succinct definition of marketing. Personally this is not my favorite definition because it is less focused on the relationship with clients and more focused on a trading process where tools such as communication, pricing and creating value are centered.

"Marketing is the science and art of exploring, creating, and delivering value to satisfy the needs of a target market at a profit. Marketing identifies unfulfilled needs and desires. It

defines measures and quantifies the size of the identified market and the profit potential. It pinpoints which segments the company is capable of serving best and it designs and promotes the appropriate products and services." – **Philip Kotler**

This old fashioned, scholastic definition is pretty accurate and comprehensive. Kotler prefers speaking of a target market instead of customers in this definition. Where other marketers would advocate the social and relational aspect of marketing, Kotler puts the emphasis on profit and profit potential, making his definition more pragmatic. Marketing being a form of art can be questioned; the fact is that marketing is more than a scientific formula in which talented marketers certainly can make a difference compared to their less talented colleagues. This difference can be found, amongst others, in having the intangible instinct, the skill to be creative *and* the talent to assess people and therefore markets, to analyze and to interpret and combine all this acquired information allow the marketer to touch the hearts of (potential) clients in an authentic way.

"Marketing is the process of developing, pricing, promoting and distributing products, services or ideas that are tailored to the market; it includes all other activities that create value and systematically lead to increased sales or another desired response, establish a good reputation and ongoing relationships with customers, so that all stakeholders achieve their objectives " – **From 'Marketing Fundamentals - An International Perspective' - By Bronis Verhage**

The base fort his definition is the classical marketing mix existing of the famous 4 P's (price, promotion, place and product), adding "new insights" such as building lasting customer relationships or pursuing a good reputation. Besides the relational aspect, emphasis is also placed on the business side of marketing which focuses on fostering transaction and increasing sales.

Marketing is not only promotion (advertising), but all activities that contribute to bringing a product or a service to the attention of a consumer, that promotes demand on the market and that ensures that ultimately a transaction takes place between the provider of a product or service and the consumer. This is done by anticipating the need of this consumer.

Chapter 3

Marketing and yoga?

The purity of yoga is – at first sight – in sharp contrast with the harsh business world that we know. I would like to point out once and for all that you do not have to compromise your values to be able to fill your studio with enthusiastic yoga students. Learn to infuse your marketing strategy with the philosophy of yoga and your personal values and norms. Make room for abundance and follow your senses. Trust me, the rest comes naturally. And the best marketing is, what else could it be, authentic marketing.

Use the yamas and the niyamas, the two limbs of Patanjali's eightfold path; they will give you guidance. Virtues such as honesty, sobriety, purity, nonviolence, compassion, should be criteria for your marketing approach.

Finding your own voice is a necessary condition to market your yoga class or –studio. As mentioned before, authenticity is the permanent ingredient in the marketing mix. Remember: there are no shortcuts to real success!

One of the paths to more success is having a marketing strategy. Everyone decides his own definition of success, but this book is about **attracting more clients permanently**. Therefore, my definition of success is that your yoga studio is financially healthy because you succeed in continuously attracting sufficient students.

Not only new students are important but the faithful visitors are possibly even more important. To know what your destination is, makes the journey to the destination easier and more focused. Having a goal, gives you purpose. A strategy, a plan, existing of several ways and means, to reach your goals. Creating a strategy will allow you to see what doesn't need focus and therefore gives you more time and means to spend on the matters that matter most.

Imagine there are four yoga studios in the area that merely offer vinyasa classes. If you would offer vinyasa classes as well, you would all be fishing in the same (potential) student pond. However it could be that you have your own unique style that appeals to many students, making your unique style a USP – or *unique selling point* –. In other words you offer something unique that appeals to many students and makes them come to your specific studio or class. But imagine that the level of the vinyasa yoga teachers in these four studios is equal; that would make it a challenge to activate people to come to your studio. Later in this book I will address tactics (possible ways and means) to reach your strategy, but you will probably already know that promotion, your pricing, the location, your teaching method, the offer, the atmosphere in the studio etc. are determining and distinguishing factors in a competitive market. In our example the owner of the studio could consider to expand its range with pregnancy yoga making the pond bigger with a new, unexplored territory. Or the studio owner has to trust that his or her teaching style is unique and attractive enough to distinguish itself from other studios, filling its classes with enthusiastic students all by itself.

Your strategy could also be to offer *less* yoga styles instead of offering several different ones. Instead of expanding the range, you reduce it. There are, undoubtedly, yoga studios that offer several styles of yoga to be able to attract a larger crowd. For some studios, this can be the right strategy to attract more students, whereas for other studios this strategy can end up giving a boomerang effect since it will mean that more styles include more teaching space, more qualified teachers with the right know-how, more need for planning, inevitably more administration, higher rent costs for using more space or several spaces, higher costs of materials as a result of expansion, etc. If, subsequently, the expected crowd stays out and you can't fill up your classes, the calculation for the end of the month income is quickly done. Going back to the essence of your studio's main activity (in this case offering a maximum of 1 or 2 styles) therefore isn't a failure but a courageous, smart and business decision resulting in getting a grip on the business side of your studio, allowing it to grow healthily.

We quickly highlighted the power of a *unique selling point (USP)* earlier. Something that distinguishes you from the other yoga studios that are located in the same area and aims for the same students as you. Your USP doesn't always have to be related to the yoga styles that you may or may not offer or the different niche markets (pregnant women, students, men, recovering cancer patients, the elderly, and children) that you want to reach. You can resolutely decide to offer healthy, fresh juices in your studio. Your yoga students can thus take a breather and have a chat or get to know each other. Moreover these juices allow you to earn a little extra money and it will contribute to the atmosphere in the yoga studio.

Again, there is no easy way to success. On the contrary, the way to the proverbial top – a top that is determined different by each and every one of us – is steep and narrow. Sometimes, success depends of matters that are intangible such as the atmosphere of your studio, how students experience your teaching style, or how full studios attract even more students because "full" is synonymous with "good". Later in this book I will elaborate on possible tactics to render intangible matters (such as atmosphere in the studio and perception of your teaching style and yoga studio) visible for your students and yourself, allowing you to follow the path to your destination with eyes wide open.

Chapter 4

DO YOU HAVE A STRATEGY?

Did you also "just" dive in head first once you made the decision to open a yoga studio, or did you write down your goals beforehand to determine the image of your yoga studio, you future students, etc.

I don't doubt you have spent a lot of time thinking about the things you want and the things you definitely do not want to do with your yoga studio. But have you also thought about the advantages and core values you want to offer to your future clients? Who these clients are, and who they aren't? What makes your studio unique or distinctive? Which possible revenue streams do you want to tap into? It's fantastic if you already thoroughly worked this out for yourself, before starting out. Maybe this chapter will just be a brush up, a check to see if you still focus on the right matters, or maybe this chapter is an opportunity to evaluate whether you need to make some changes to your current approach. If you haven't had this practice yet, you can use the following instructions to better understand yourself, your studio and your (future) customers. These instructions will give you a foundation to further build once your insight grows, making it clear and bright what your destination (strategy) is, how you can obtain it (your tactics or the difficult paths you may walk on) and what you will need for it (your means such as time and money).

The lack of a strategy is like traveling without a destination. It's important to have a direction during your travels so as to be able to reach your destination. It's not that you won't be flexible if suddenly an opportunity or unseen circumstance emerges, just because you have an itinerary. If you notice that the destination you had imagined for yourself is not as attractive as you had first imagined, it is still possible to change your direction. Having a destination and a plan to reach this destination allows your eyes to be focused on your destination and allows you to make the right decisions faster during your journey. In other words, you have a focus and you don't have to worry that the destination and direction that you have mapped out are set in stone.

4.1. Do you know your target group?
Again, I won't get into the details of marketing theories in this book. If you want to know more about demographic, social-economic, geographic, psycho-graphic features of a target group, how to chart these and how this target group is subdivided (segmented) into niche markets, then I would like to refer you to the earlier mentioned literature or our best Internet friend, Google.

I would like to give you a few examples to clarify that knowing your target audience or the people you want to direct your message to ("come do yoga at my studio") will offer lots of benefits.

Segmenting the consumers market will allow you to subdivide the entire market into smaller, sharply contoured markets, niche markets or segments. By dividing the market into segments (a group of potential customers with the same features) you can approach "your" potential group of customers in a better way because you know them better on the one hand, and on the other hand they show specific features that allow you to approach them easier. By knowing who you are aiming at, you are able to adapt your communication to your target audience or choose your location which will make it easy for your target audience to find you. Also, you will know where you have to be to spread your marketing message.

Imagine you teach yoga classes for children. Wouldn't it be interesting to know in which parts of the city or region the most children can be found, and in which areas you won't find any? Imagine, on the other hand, that you need to focus your business yoga classes on employees of companies, making it interesting to find out in which part of the area you can find a large concentration of employees, and opening your studio there.

Or you could distinguish yourself from the other yoga centers with an exclusive offer focused on students, which would make it wise to open the studio in a student residential area. Knowing who you want to focus on, which people you want to attract, helps in communicating to target audience. Subsequently, you do not approach pregnant women in the same way you would students. In order to trigger students to come to your yoga class, you could leave flayers in the student areas spreading the word that yoga is the perfect hangover remedy after a night out, mentioning several benefits why yoga helps relieve the hangover. Pregnant women on the other hand would be more drawn to a message that shows that yoga during pregnancy helps with breathing and relaxing, which in turn helps with the physical challenges involved in bringing a baby in the world.

You don't have to show a complicated analysis or gather tons of data to establish who you want to target and who therefore belongs to your target group. Of course you want to aim at "everybody" because yoga offers benefits to everybody. This train of thought is a beautiful principle and I hope wholeheartedly that you will manage to get "everybody" to your studio. The reality, however, is that not every person is interested in yoga, so I would advise against the idea to adapt your communication to "everybody". Targeted communication to a specific target audience will save you time, money, frustration, and moreover a targeted communication will allow you to actually reach the audience you want to reach.

TIP: Take a bit of time and try to sketch a profile of your current students and of the people you are trying to reach. There is no such thing as one, exact profile. You probably have different profiles in your studio, but mapping them will give insight to which profiles (and thus which characteristics) are most strongly represented. These characteristics can be external features such as obese people, pregnant women or toned men, but can also be characteristics such as education level, residence, professional situation, age, gender, personality, etc. The characteristics can give you insight so that, at a later stage, you can better coordinate your marketing activities to the desired target audience.

4.2. Do you know your competition?

No matter how you look at it, analyzing what other yoga studios do when it comes to marketing, decoration, classes, workshops, rates, etc. provides you with a competitive advantage. I suggest that you identify who your competitors are and to analyze them.

❑ *Where are your competitors? Do you know your competitors?*

A yoga studio is a local matter. Yoga enthusiasts do not want to travel for hours and thus prefer to choose a studio in the immediate vicinity. There's a strong possibility that you will have to work harder to attract students if you open your studio close to another studio as opposed to opening a studio in an area where there is no yoga-offer yet.
Do you know all your competitors?

❑ *Which audience(s) does your competitors target?*

Do they all offer Vinyasa yoga and is there no Iyengar, Ashtanga or Hatha yoga being taught? Is there a studio that focuses on students, the elderly or pregnant women?

❑ *What are their strengths? What are their weaknesses?*
Don't be embarrassed to take several classes with competitors and establish their strengths and their weaknesses.

❑ *Which products and/or services do they offer?*
For example, a yoga studio that has a yoga shop in addition to offering classes, and sells yoga products such as mats, blocks, straps, etc. Besides this complementary offer, I also recommend analyzing which yoga styles your competitors practice. If they all offer Vinyasa classes, it might be a good opportunity to offer Iyengar or any other styles of yoga classes.

❑ *Are they hygienic?*
This question might seem unnecessary at first, but looking further, you will notice that the cleanliness of a yoga studio contributes to the total yoga-experience of a client in your studio. If you go out for dinner and have a great meal, only to establish that the toilets are filthy and disgusting after visiting them, your total restaurant-experience will be negative. Although you don't go to a restaurant for the toilets, it is important that they are clean to make your experience a positive one.
On the other hand, a clean toilet won't be a reason to recommend a restaurant to your friends and acquaintances. The same goes for your own studio or your competition.

❑ *Are there any dressing rooms?*
Another question that doesn't seem important at first, but I can assure you that some students prefer a separate dressing room where they can change in private to having to get (un)dressed in front of other students. Of course there are students that don't care about this at all. Getting changed surrounded by other people can contribute to the atmosphere in your studio, just like having separate dressing rooms. Unless you see that many students drop out of your classes because they don't like having to change in public, my advice would be to follow your heart. Nevertheless, it is appropriate to

check out the competitors to see how they tackle this issue and ask your students whether they find this important.

❑ *What are their prices?*
Do they use subscriptions and punch cards? Do they give discounts? When and to whom? How much does a student pay for one class? Do they have free trial classes for new students? Do you find them expensive or cheap or are their rates appropriate for what they offer? Obviously it's not easy to objectively evaluate their offer, but try to have a chat with the students that you meet when visiting a yoga studio in your neighborhood, and inquire about their experiences.

❑ *How is the atmosphere in the studio?*
Atmosphere is something intangible, but having a good atmosphere or lacking one is something you sense immediately. Assess your competition based on the atmosphere in their studio and try to make this intangible differentiator tangible. How do you feel about the decoration? How are you welcomed? How is the atmosphere during class? Are people laughing, or is everyone very serious? Is the room too hot or too cold?

❑ *What do you think of the location?*
Is the studio well located? Is it easily accessible or is there a lot of traffic? Are their (free) parking spaces in the area? You ask these questions to rank competing studios according to their location on the one hand, but on the other hand they also enable you to reflect on your own location.

❑ *Do they organize workshops and/or retreats?*
Offering workshops and/or retreats can provide a competitive advantage because it allows you to aim at yoga enthusiasts that want to deepen their yoga practice.

❑ *How do they advertise?*
Which communication channels do your competitors use? Do they have a website? Do they place online advertisements? Do they sponsor events in the neighborhood? Do you find

their flyers at the local bakery and butcher shop? How do you think they rank in the field of advertisement?

❑ *What is their market share?*
If you would have to estimate how many yoga practitioners reside in your area, what percentage of these yoga practitioners go to studio X and what percentage go to studio Y? Is there a percentage of the yoga practitioners that is not loyal and that visit different studios? If you know how large the entire pie is and which studio owns which slice of the pie (market share), then it's up to you to determine how large you envision your piece of that pie to be in relation to other studios.

❑ *How do you see the market evolving in the future?*
Are there other yogis that are likely to open up a studio in your area? Would it make sense to join forces? Are there any possible threats that may emerge in the future which might put you in a difficult situation? It may be smart to check with the municipality to make sure that there are no major maintenance works scheduled in the vicinity of your yoga studio, ensuring its accessibility.

Without a doubt there must be at least another dozen of relevant issues that come to mind or that you find important to analyze concerning your competition.
A useful tool to map your competitors is a simple table containing the names of your competitors in the first column. In the second, third and fourth column you can rate topics that you find important (price, hygiene, offer of styles, dressing rooms, etc...) when it comes to competitors, using the topics from the above list as an inspiration.

See example:

Name studio	Pricing	Hygiene	Quality of classes	Class offer	Styles
X	+	+	++	-	-
Y	+	+	++	+	-
Z	+	+	-	-	-

From the above table you can see, for example, that none of the yoga studios score high on offering different yoga styles. A yoga studio that offers more yoga styles or different styles of yoga could prove to be an interesting addition.

TIP: constantly analyzing the performance of your competition will help you to promptly catch or anticipate possible threats. Moreover, it allows you to position your studio in such a way that you can increase your chances on success. By positioning I mean that you search for those traits that distinguish you from your competition and that you make clear choices as to what you do and do not want for you studio. Good positioning means that - although there are many other yoga studios – you anticipate the needs of the target audience(s) in your market segment in a unique way.

4.3. Do you know what your Unique Selling Proposition (USP) is?

In which areas do you differentiate or do you want to differentiate from the other yoga studios in the neighborhood? What are your unique assets - apart from your rates - that you and only you can offer? Why should I follow my weekly yoga class with you? What story do you have to tell?

An example of how you can distinguish yourself is the manner in and frequency with which you give students adjustments to perform their poses. A cozy yoga studio can consciously decide – so as to set themselves apart from the big yoga centers - to pay extra attention to the students that visit the studio in order to give these students the feeling that they are really being supported and that they - especially beginners - come into a pose correctly. You can also differentiate yourself by paying extra attention to the meditative aspect which allows students to learn meditation in addition to yoga, or you could distinguish yourself by also offering fresh juices in a chill corner where students (and possibly teachers) can meet and enjoy themselves.

Attention: I would like to remind you that these are merely ideas, not a recipe for guaranteed success. Follow your heart and let yourself be inspired by the *yamas* and *niyamas*.

Do you know what you and your studio stand for? What are your core values (your ethical compass) that can be found in your approach, service and offer?
Calibrating your ethical compass is crucial. If you know what it is you stand for and which core values are important to you, then you also know what you definitely do not want. This will give you more focus and taking decisions will become easier. You can, for example, attach a lot of value to the care for your students. This entails that you will make it your business that everyone cleans their mat after class - if they lend or rent - and puts them back into the appropriate place. It also means that you pro-actively reach out to a student with a monthly subscription who has been absent for two weeks due to illness or an accident, offering them two weeks of free classes upon return. Can you imagine how this student will feel when you give him the good news? Do you think he/she will share his positive experience with friends and acquaintances? Indeed, your gesture is not only caring but is also a boost of satisfaction for this student who will undoubtedly spread the word and might motivate new students to come and visit your studio.

Have you thought about how your students will feel after a visit to your studio?

How would you like students to think about your yoga-offer and the studio?

Receiving feedback from your students is a golden opportunity to improve. Many people confuse feedback with criticism, and do not take the opportunity to learn from it. Embrace feedback and don't take criticism personally, but consider it to be a personal opinion -and therefore perception- about what it is you have to offer. People are not naturally inclined to express their opinion to the same person it pertains to. Therefore, encourage your students to give feedback on your classes but also on how they experience the studio. This doesn't mean that you should immediately do something with this feedback, but it at least is a first step to (personal and business) growth. You could, for example, send a short online survey to students that visited your studio for the first time, in order to measure their experience regarding your class, your studio, the atmosphere, etc. Or you could place a suggestion box at a neutral place (the entrance?) which can visually encourage your students to share their ideas with you.

Besides mapping your own USP's, I recommend to also map those of your competition. Knowing the unique strengths of your competition helps you position yourself (see 4.4. Do you know your competition?).

TIP: make a (short)list of your assets and determine on which level your yoga studio distinguishes itself from the other studios (in your vicinity). Attach your core values to it; the ones you wish to implement for yourself, your students, your employees, volunteers, etc. Your assets and your core values complement each other and therefore form the basis of your unique selling proposition. In other words, they represent all that you and you studio stand for.

Also use this exercise to have your assets and core values convey the approach you have envisioned for the future.

4.4. How did you determine your rates?

Many yoga fanatics argue that the pursuit of money is contradictory to the value that yoga philosophy embraces. Let's be honest, starting your own yoga studio is not only for the sake of your students, but also for yourself. In exchange for your services, students pay money that allows you to keep your studio going and also provides for you and your family.

What price should I charge? Do I give discounts? Do I offer subscriptions? Do I work with monthly-, quarterly-, or yearly subscriptions? Undoubtedly, these are either the most difficult or the easiest questions that you have to answer when opening your yoga studio. Often it happens that entrepreneurs, which you are, look at their competitors and base their own rates on those of the competition. After all, you are scared that, if your rates are too high, the studio stays empty. But at the same time you're struggling with the pricing pressure because the price of a yoga class offers your company the proverbial oxygen that it needs to exist.

Have you ever wondered why the price of a lunch menu at a fancy restaurant is much higher than the 5-course menu at the Chinese restaurant around the corner? Even though both restaurants offer good food. Who or what decides that one restaurant offers a meal for $30, whereas the other offers it for $300? You surely have an idea what determines the pricing of the menus at these restaurants. This exercise can be used for your yoga studio as well. It might make sense to have a slightly higher rate than your closest competitor if this fits the audience that you seek to attract, or if you believe that your class is worth it. There are certainly students that are more than happy to pay a bit more because they feel connected to the decoration of your studio, or because you offer them personal adjustments during class.

Maybe you should take a bigger risk and give classes for free, or even based on donations. This - at first sight - radical approach could become one of your USP's in the long run and, moreover, teaching free or donation-based classes doesn't necessarily mean that you earn less of a living. Free classes may not be recommended if you rent your own space, buy your material and want to provide for your family. It may be an idea to give free classes every Saturday and Sunday afternoon in a park, at the beach on in a local fitness center, before you open your own studio. This way you lower the threshold to attend your yoga classes. This approach could help you introduce yourself as a yoga teacher to a large audience. A steady number of yoga enthusiasts will gladly follow you to your own studio. Asking a voluntary donation for your yoga class is also an idea that could, on the one hand, allow you to estimate how many people value your class and, on the other hand, such a pricing pattern gives people with limited financial means the opportunity to join in on classes. You could, for example, advertise at the entrance of your studio that the recommended donation for a class is around $20 Euro, and approximately $10 for university students. You could also emphasize that you find it important that the studio is accessible for everybody and that a donation is completely voluntary. I however find it important that you openly communicate that, without donations, you cannot guarantee that your studio can be kept open in the long run. In other words, encourage your students to donate if they believe that the classes you teach helps or means something to them.

The most straightforward way of determining a correct rate is by mapping your expenses and calculating how many students you need at a specific rate to be able to cover all expenses every month (including your salary). Besides this straightforward pricing you can ask yourself 4 questions:

1. How much would your ideal customer be willing to pay for a visit to your studio?
Remember, you are NOT your ideal customer simply because your services are not an added value to you personally. Ultimately, the person who will be offering the services is you! Your yoga class offers a tremendous value to your ideal customer and this customer knows how to appreciate it. This is the main reason that students are willing to pay for a class.

Set your prices too low and you're selling yourself short, running the risk of students questioning your classes. They will question your expertise or they will doubt your ability to teach them. Your rates do also determine the perception that people have of your studio.

2. Do you know how much you have to earn each month to keep your studio running in a sustainable and healthy way?
A business plan should help you determine the budget necessary to open up your yoga studio, to decorate it and to run it on a monthly basis. It is also important to prepare a worst-case and best-case scenario in which you calculate how many students are willing to pay, for example, $20 per class enabling you to pay your monthly loans, wages, commercial-expenses, rent, etc. If you set the price per class too low, you will have to attract an unrealistic amount of yoga-enthusiasts or you will have to teach an impossible amount of classes. Set your prices too high and your students won't show up.

3. Are you considerate towards your competitors?
I can already hear you thinking: "why would I be considerate towards my competitors?". An important rule when it comes to competition is that **when you compete at price-level, nobody wins**. Setting your rates too low will put pressure on your competitors' rates who might in turn start cutting their prices as well. This is a dead end street and at the end of it, you will have driven each other out of business, maintaining such low rates that nobody is able to make enough money to keep a financially healthy studio opened. Rates can never be a USP, so find your unique, personal assets and decide what your ideal customer would be willing to pay for this.

4. Does your competition offer a membership structure that you don't?
As with many yoga studios you can pay per class or you can purchase a punch cards or even a monthly-, quarterly-, or yearly subscription to take unlimited classes during the agreed period. My advice would be to take a closer look at the membership structure, because not offering such a

subscription for the yoga enthusiast who intensively practices yoga could potentially be a reason for this student to go to your competitor.

The price-setting process is like walking on a high-wire across a river. Finding balance is crucial in order to reach the other side. Keep in mind that only you know the answer to the question which price you should ask your students. Having insight and knowing how rates can be determined and influenced is a good step towards a financially healthy yoga studio. If you would like to know more about pricing strategies, price elasticity and the influence of your rates on your income, I recommend the following book:

- "The Strategy and Tactics of Pricing: A Guide to Growing More Profitably" - by Thomas Nagle

TIP: Check what your competitors charge and which membership structure they offer. Analyze your expenses and calculate how many students and/or classes you need at a specific price per class to be able to cover these expenses. Also try to keep the market healthy by not setting your prices too low, ensuring that the pricing pressure you put on your competition won't come back to strike you like a boomerang. Find your own balance and figure out which assets and values you offer to your students and what they are worth to them.

Chapter 5

Goals give direction

In previous chapters you were introduced to the basic principles of marketing. Now you can start analyzing your target audience, your competitors, your unique and therefore distinctive assets (USP's), your rates, etc. These basic principles combined form the beginning of your marketing plan. As mentioned before, knowing what you want and don't want, having a goal, will help you focus. How to cover the distance and what is needed for this, will be discussed in the next chapter.

Buckle up and prepare yourself for the ride of your life!
Imagine, you set travelling as your goal. The first thing you will do is map out what you need to make this trip. You carefully pick your destination. Maybe you have to book different flights, take a few transfers, plan a boat trip, find places to stay, buy a new suitcase...

Your tickets have been booked and you're ready to start the most adventurous trip of your life. When you arrive at the airport to check in, you find that your flight has been cancelled. Focused on reaching your destination, you go towards the info desk and check when the next flight is planned. That's when they explain that the first flight isn't going to leave for another 2 days. It doesn't throw you off balance, however, and you book the next flight. Once home, you feel calm. Knowing what your destination is and wanting to reach it no matter what, strengthens your faith in having a positive outcome. You accept that you'll reach the destination two days later than planned and turn this negative experience into a positive one.

These two additional days now give you the opportunity to prepare yourself even better for the adventure that awaits you. Two days later you once again check in at the airport and this time around, everything goes smoothly! You drop off your luggage, continue toward passport control, you easily pass security and moments later you find yourself in the comfortable seat of a Boeing 737 on your way to the first transfer where you have to wait another 4 hours or so for your next flight.

The engines are running at full capacity now and through the crackling speakers you hear the captains' voice. The plane gradually starts to move and slowly approaches the runway. The cabin crew quickly give the safety instructions and ten minutes later you're already up in the air. Your first flight takes about fifteen hours and you decide to rest your eyes and enjoy your favorite music. Time flies and so do you. Fifteen hours later you are - as announced by the captain upon departure - on your first destination. Flying for fifteen hours takes its toll and once you disembark the plane you decide to stretch your legs while waiting for your next flight. You visit the tax-free shops, you eat a vegetarian snack (what else?) and you read your book. After four hours, you're aboard the next flight towards your tropical island, arriving at your destination a mere eight hours later.

Setting goals is much like traveling. You cannot expect that everything will go as planned and reaching your destination demands patience, perseverance and focus. In our day-to-day lives, we constantly set ourselves goals that lead us to the destinations we have in mind. Your goal might be to run a marathon or to spend quality time with a good friend every month, to open up a yoga studio, or to go swimming with your daughter every week... In other words: goals give meaning to your life. They will act as a guide you once you've defined what they are. Be careful: goals are not the same as wishes, good resolutions or intentions. Whereas an intention or wish is non-committal, a goal is determinative.

As you set goals for yourself, you should also set them for your yoga studio. This way you make sure that you are headed in the "right" direction with you yoga studio, and that you won't get lost on the way. Goals are fully realized when they are formulated in a SMART way.

Specific (S)
The more specific an objective is, the less you will deviate from it.

A clear objective answers the Five W's:
1. What do you want to achieve in concrete terms?
2. Who is involved in realizing your objective?
3. Where does it happen?
4. When does it happen?
5. Why do you want to reach that specific objective?

For example: our objective is to teach more yoga classes at an average of $20 per class:
1. What? Minimum of 10 yoga classes per week at an average of $20 per class
2. Who? Me
3. Where? 5 private classes and 5 classes at a local fitness center
4. When? In a period of 3 months
5. Why? Making a living out of my passion

Measurable (M)
To measure is to know. By making your objective specific you will make it measurable. This allows you to monitor how close you are to reaching your objective, and you will know when you've obtained it. In the example above it is perfectly measurable when we have reached our goal: once we have taught a minimum of 10 yoga classes at an average of $20 per class after 3 months.

Achievable (A)

It is important that people who are given an objective, also accept this objective. If there is not enough support for the objective, then it will not be reached. If you give other people objectives, I suggest that you involve them in formulating the objective to make sure they support and therefore accept it themselves. If you give yourself an objective, it is imperative that you believe in it yourself. In our example, it is imperative that the person who teaches, really wants to do this for him- or herself.

Realistic (R)

You should always ask yourself if your objective is attainable. If you haven't yet succeeded teaching a single yoga class and your purpose is to teach 10 classes within 3 months, your objective is most likely not very realistic. In short, you must be honest with yourself. It is important that you make a correct estimation of your objective so that you can both be challenged and motivated to reach your objective at the same time. Sometimes it's better to take small steps that are realistic, rather than taking 1 big step that is unrealistic. **Success motivates, even if it is a "small" success**.

Time bound (T)

A good objective always has a specific start date and an end date. This way you can follow the progress that has been made. By giving yourself a deadline, you oblige yourself to focus on the objective that lies ahead. To be able to teach 10 classes with an average price of $20, you would do good to give yourself the time to get those 10 classes. An action plan with clear points of action and a target date can help you reach your goal.

You don't have to set 10 targets for yourself or your yoga studio; that's not how it works. Pursuing too many goals is not realistic anyway. I would advise to set 2-3 goals every six months and work on those in a focused way in order to achieve them.

With regards to setting goals, I would like to refer you to a few books that have inspired me:

- "Do It! or Ditch It: Turn Ideas into Action and Make Decisions that Count"- by Bev James
- "Think and Grow Rich" - by Napoleon Hill
- "The Principle of the Path: How to Get from Where You Are to Where You Want to Be" - by Andy Stanley
- "Goals!: How to Get Everything You Want Faster Than You Ever Thought Possible" - by Brian Tracy
- "The Monk Who Sold His Ferrari: A Fable About Fulfilling Your Dreams & Reaching Your Destiny" - by Robin S. Sharma

Chapter 6

Action!

Which goals do you want to reach for your yoga studio? The list below containing general goals, - which you can turn into SMART goals yourself - can be used as inspiration to set objectives for your studio:

- ❑ Attracting more yoga enthusiasts to your studio
- ❑ Attracting more people that have never practiced yoga
- ❑ Attracting people from specific fields of sports (runners, swimmers, soccer players)
- ❑ Selling more monthly-, quarterly-, yearly memberships (unlimited yoga for a specific period) or (in other words) attracting more intensively practicing yogis
- ❑ Attracting clients from a niche market (pregnant women, men, children, recovering cancer patients, people with back problems)
- ❑ Offering more yoga classes
- ❑ Offering a broader spectrum of classes
- ❑ Opening a web shop with yoga products
- ❑ Offering more workshops, events and/or retreats
- ❑ Offering a yoga teacher training
- ❑ Starting a yoga shop in your studio
- ❑ Opening a juice bar in your studio
- ❑ Increasing the average expenditure per visitor at your yoga studio

All above objectives are objectives that can be traced back to the *main goal* why companies (and therefore you and your yoga studio) use marketing. The main goal is to attract more visitors to your studio who will subsequently spend more money on one or several of the products or services you offer. You will respond to the needs of your (potential) clients or target audience by analyzing and understanding your target audiences on the one hand, and using the different on- and offline marketing tools to communicate your message to your (present/future) target audience(s) on the other hand. With this main goal in mind, we will discuss practical tips and *marketing tools* that can help you develop your yoga studio, in the following chapters.

Chapter 7

Practical tips & marketing tools

I try to make the tips and tools that I offer in this book as concrete as possible so that they are ready to use and easily put into practice. Sometimes, however, it isn't possible to explain all the details or a specific process completely because of the complexity of the matter or because it goes beyond the objective of this book: inspiring and supporting yoga entrepreneurs in the development of their studio. In these cases I refer to websites, books, people or specialized companies that can help you further with the subject. It goes without saying that you can always contact me in case you'd like to have more information on a specific subject or if you find I haven't sufficiently covered it. All your questions, suggestions, feedback or fan mail ☺ is welcome at mathieu.van.steenberge@gmail.com.
Namaste!

7.1. Branding your yoga studio?

The term "branding" finds its origin in the days when farmers used to brand their cattle. This way, farmers could easily identify their own cattle. This is exactly what large, medium sized and small companies do. They distinguish themselves from each other and from their competition by giving their company a face, by branding. For many this face is a logo, but if we dig deeper we can confirm that branding is much more than simply an original and visually attractive logo.

On the Internet I found the following definitions on branding:

"A name, term, design, symbol, or any other feature that identifies one seller's good or service as distinct from those of other sellers. The legal term for brand is trademark. A brand may identify one item, a family of items, or all items of that seller. If used for the firm as a whole, the preferred term is trade name." - **The American Marketing Association**

"A brand is the set of expectations, memories, stories and relationships that, taken together, account for a consumer's decision to choose one product or service over another. If the consumer (whether it's a business, a buyer, a voter or a donor) doesn't pay a premium, make a selection or spread the word, then no brand value exists for that consumer." - **Seth Godin**

"A brand is a name, term, sign, symbol, or design or a combination of them, intended to identify the goods and services of one seller or group of sellers and to differentiate them from those of the competitor." - **Phillip Kotler**

"A brand is the intangible sum of a product's attributes: its name, packaging, and price, its history, its reputation, and the way it's advertised." - **David Ogilvy**

"The process involved in creating a unique name and image for a product in the consumers' mind, mainly through advertising campaigns with a consistent theme. Branding aims to establish a significant and differentiated presence in the market that attracts and retains loyal customers." - **businessdictionary.com**

As you can deduce from the above definitions, branding is the sum of everything you say, do and undertake, together contributing to the uniqueness and visibility of your enterprise.

In this chapter I discuss concrete tips & tricks to give your yoga studio a face so that your studio will stand out and also to allow you to be unique in your approach. Adding your own style to your studio contributes to the growth of your studio in the short and long term. Just like some faces radiate charisma, an energy or a feeling, branding will help you to create a certain sensation or atmosphere in your yoga studio. Since I want to limit myself to offering concrete tips & tricks in this chapter, I would like to refer you to specialized literature in case you would like to delve into brand management.

Books that I can recommend on this subject are:
- "Designing Brand Identity: A Complete Guide to Creating, Building, and Maintaining Strong Brands" – by Alina Wheeler
- "Brand Leadership" – by David Aaker & Erich Joachimsthaler
- "Branding For Dummies" – by Bill Chiaravalle

Branding is a series of techniques you can apply to give your company a face. Branding also contributes to what people - in the blink of an eye - think of your company. Branding plays to the emotions of people, as well as the rational side. Because people react differently to colors, a logo, a text or slogan, the combination of colors, texts, slogans, logo, decoration, teaching style, the way your newsletter looks, etc. all contribute to the brand experience of your students. Many small and medium sized enterprises feel overwhelmed by the subject of branding and there are undoubtedly many experts that are eager to advise you on building a brand. These experts costs large amounts of money and for large, established companies it is advisable to be guided by branding experts. But entrepreneurs of small businesses such as your yoga studio, remember the following tips and tricks if you wish to turn your yoga studio into a (local) brand/concept, so that people from the area will immediately think of your studio when they think of yoga.

Either way, I have good news for all yoga studio owners: you are working more at branding than you may think. You undoubtedly have a name for your studio, some may even already have a logo or work with an assortment of colors, and each of you possesses at least one unique and powerful tool: your own personality and the resulting personal and therefore authentic class style that leaves the biggest mark on your studio.

What name do you choose for your yoga studio?
If you read this book, you have probably already found a wonderful name for your studio. But it could also be that this name no longer fits you and/or your studio or that the name is so common that you have a hard time distinguishing yourself from the other studios. It's worth considering to not name your studio after a style of yoga, because this is anything but unique and you may not be the only person using this name.
Uniqueness starts with the choice of your name, so it may be advisable to really think it over.

The following tips (source: http://www.wikihow.com/Choose-a-Company-Name) could help you choose a captivating and unique name for your yoga studio.

1. Make sure that the name of your yoga studio respects the SMILE-standard:

a. Simple – choose a name that is easily spelled and that doesn't cause any confusion for people that have to remember it and/or write down the name. A word from Sanskrit can sound very attractive and may be easy to write for you, but 99% of your students don't understand Sanskrit so think twice before using a word from a different language.
b. Meaningful – a company name that also embraces the values of your company is a welcome bonus, but is not us must. The company name "Apple", for example, has been chosen by Steve Jobs because his company was facing a challenge to dethrone the competition. The competition was called Atari, among others. By choosing the name "Apple",

Jobs made sure that his company was listed above their competition in the phone book, making sure clients would knock at their door before turning to Atari. Another reason for choosing the name is that Jobs used to work at an apple orchard in Oregon of which he kept fond memories.

c. Imagery – it is advantageous that your name evokes an image to your customers. Images stimulate fantasy, and fantasy includes sentiment (also see point e. "Emotional"). In other words, your name can evoke certain emotions in (potential) clients.

d. Legs – your name must be strong and clear enough so that you can use different angles when communicating with your clients.

e. Emotional – a name that raises positive emotions, is always a welcome addition.

2. Ignore any name that meets the SCRATCH-standard:

a. Spelling-challenged – don't use a name that is hard to spell.

b. Copycat – it's a bad idea to use a name that is similar or equivalent to your competition or similar companies. In other words, be unique!

c. Random – a random name does not bring any connection to you or your yoga studio and therefore it is better to avoid a random name.

d. Annoying – a name that is forced or annoying, will not encourage your target audience to visit your studio.

e. Tame – a boring name, missing inspiration and passion, is not advisable.

f. Curse of knowledge – try to not get lost in the yoga terminology that is only understandable by insiders, experts or fanatics.

g. Hard to pronounce – stay away from a name that is difficult to pronounce or that needs extra attention when you say/write it.

3. General advice:

a. Brainstorm – take a brainstorm session and let your ideas on the loose. Note every name that pops up in your head.
b. Evaluate & eliminate – consider the SIMPLE-standard and the SCRATCH-standard. Try to select which names qualify and which don't, based on these two standards.
c. Ask for feedback – your students are a source of wisdom, so ask them what they think of the ideas for names that you have. Let them choose which name speaks most to them.

Moms and dads that read this book, will certainly agree that choosing a name is an important decision. Just as you cannot change the name of your child, you would be wise to chose the name of your studio with necessary consideration, because the name of your studio will be mentioned innumerable times.

You have your name, now you need a logo!
Now that you have decided on a name, you need to consider letting this name come to life by using a logo. Your logo decides, among others, the atmosphere your studio radiates and therefore forms a visual representation of your studio. Having a logo made, or making it yourself, is not an easy feat. Your name and logo decides the atmosphere your yoga studio breathes.

Below tips can help you make the right choice when it comes to choosing a logo or having one designed.

Ask yourself the following things:

1. Does the design of the logo fit you and your target audience?
Do you remember your core values? Do you have the option to add one or more values to the design of your logo? You could, for example, decide to give the logo a distinct green color so as to add the value of "ecologic business". After all, the color green exudes ecology and through colors you can

evoke a certain ambiance or certain values with your target group.

2. What do you want to say or achieve?
Your logo is your visual representation, and just like your name will be pronounced by your (potential) clients numerous times, your logo will be seen numerous times by your (potential) clients.

3. How will your logo be reproduced?
Will your logo mostly be used as black-and-white copies? Then it might be smart to design a black-and-white logo. Is your logo supposed to be magnified, then it might be wise not to make your logo too complex.

4. What are your limitations?
Do you have a budget in mind? Do you have specific requirements you do not want to deviate from? Are there legal limitations? Researching your limitations and clearly mapping them, is advisable if you want to start off with a professional logo.

5. Which atmosphere do you want to radiate?
The color, the image(s), the size, and the font all determine the atmosphere that the logo and therefore your studio radiate.

6. Do you want a slogan?
A good slogan could reinforce the visual character of your logo. Ask yourself whether you find a slogan important or not. Also think about the use of the slogan when reproducing your logo for marketing purposes. Does the slogan fit the wall sign above the entrance of your studio? Does the slogan fit on your business card?

You can also consider documenting decisions in a style guide, when it comes to your logo, name and atmosphere. A style guide has many advantages, such as monitoring uniformity and making decisions easier to take. This way you don't have to doubt which colors you have to use or the tone of voice to use for an ad.

Do you want to know how to set up such a guide? Read the following article:
http://designshack.net/articles/graphics/how-to-build-a-brand-bible-visual-style-guide

Are you looking for someone to design your logo? Maybe www.99designs.be or www.freelancer.com could be something for you! You can put several designers to work and choose the best design at a competitive price.

Using your name and logo in your communication.
Your name and logo are fixed elements that are always addressed in communication with your clients.

1. Name cards or business cards
Remember that business cards leave and impression on the person to whom you give it., Therefore, ask yourself which impression you would like to leave. You could choose to have a "playful" and creative business card designed, or you can choose to have a standard business card printed.

The business card below was designed by Danielle Abisaab, a yoga teacher from Beirut
http://www.cardonizer.com/business_cards/danielle_abisaab

A straw as a business card?
https://www.pinterest.com/pin/270497521342346756

Business cards with yoga asanas?
http://us.moo.com/design-templates/business-cards/pack/yoga-poses.html

Also check
http://cardobserver.com/gallery/yoga-business-cards-2

2. Sponsoring industry events

Industry events, local or other, are an ideal occasion to put your studio in the spotlight. Imagine spontaneous initiatives in your city, village or community to put people in motion. Participate in local events that are involved with sports and/or health.

3. Promotional material

Do not expect that sharing promotional material will suddenly give you an influx of new students. Promotional material mostly works as a support for your name- and logo publicity. This publicity will make sure that you stay top-of-mind.

Promotional material that could be efficient to promote your studio:
Stress balls
Ballpoint pens
Water bottles
Yoga mat bags
Reusable hot- and cold packs

4. Mobilizing your logo

Using your logo, helps to create a bigger name- and logo publicity. Places where it is advisable to use your name and logo:

- ❑ **Website** – your website is your online business card which is why your name and logo should be published on your website.
- ❑ **Personal- and team branding** – it could be advisable to "brand" the employees of your yoga studio. You can dress them with personalized t-shirts (showing their name, the name of the studio and your logo).
- ❑ **Merchandise** – promotional material with your name and logo, contributes to mobilizing/spreading and therefore increasing the visibility for your target audience.
- ❑ **Car** – placing stickers on your car is a must-do! Your car is a moving billboard and increases the visibility of

your studio in your area (which is where you find your target audience!).

☐ **Email signature & auto responders** – Every email you send out is communication and therefore an opportunity to project your logo on the retina of the receiver. Moreover, an email signature gives the opportunity to link it to your YouTube channel where you could make an online yoga workshop for beginners available.

☐ **Newsletter** – your newsletter is another form of communication and promotion. Through your newsletter you activate your audience. You make sure that your studio is once again top-of-mind, and by means of your newsletter you can pass along both information and atmosphere to your clients.

☐ **Subscription** – Do you use customer subscriptions or membership structures? Do they clearly display your name and logo? Do the colors match the atmosphere that you want to radiate?

☐ **Reception room** – the place where everybody passes is the perfect place to clearly show your name and logo.

☐ **Signings** – signs that show directions or indicate a specific location/room, can be cheered up/branded with your logo. I also suggest designing these signs in the same style as your interior.

☐ **Stationary** – although you will probably only send a limited amount of letters per mail, you could consider buying customized stationary.

What are the next steps to expand your name and logo to a strong (local) brand?

Word-of-mouth marketing and personal branding

In Chapter 7.6 I will further discuss the subject of personal branding and the link to word-of-mouth communication, but allow me to introduce to you the force of a personal brand and word-of-mouth communication.

You cannot sell yoga to people. Clients know that it is good for them and that they should do it. You must sell them something different, something only you have: the community that you create in your studio, your personal teaching style, a unique offer of eco yoga clothing...

Besides a name and logo for your yoga studio, it is equally important that your personal approach is one of your assets. This approach is crucial in building the structure of a successful studio. It is the only thing the competition cannot copy.

You can have the most eye-catching logo, the best sounding name, original business cards and a newsletter, but if your clients don't feel connected to you and your way of teaching, you'll quickly have to close the doors. **Word-of-mouth marketing is your most important form of marketing**.
If you would ask around your students and find out where they heard of you/your studio, the most heard answer would be "through a friend". The reason people recommend a product or service to other people is because they are satisfied with this product or service. In your case, your students must be satisfied about your teaching style and the feeling they have after having visited your studio. People go to a restaurant for the good food, but if you visit the toilet in this restaurant it should also be clean and pleasant.

People don't go to a restaurant for the toilets. However, when the food is delicious but the toilets are not clean, the overall feeling for this person will predominantly be negative. This comparison also works when visiting a yoga studio. The connection with the yoga teacher and the teaching style are most important, but if the studio is covered in a layer of dust this could be a reason for your students to be dissatisfied. In short, the devil is in the details. It takes time to build up a reputation, but a good reputation doesn't take much time to be destroyed. The main question is how you as a yoga teacher, can accelerate building a reputation. The answer is: by standing out, by distinguishing yourself in such a way that it is relevant for your students. This relevance will result in a connection, and this connection will in turn make sure that you build up a good reputation ensuring that your students will more easily recommend you to their friends, acquaintances and family.

You can also decide to build your reputation with a specific target audience. That way you can work in a focused manner on making a name amongst surfers, runners, people over 55, or organize a class for mothers and daughters.

Another way to reinforce your personal brand, is by offering (beginners) yoga classes on YouTube.

See below for a few examples:
❑ Kino MacGregor:
http://www.youtube.com/user/KinoYoga
❑ Yoga With Adriene:
https://www.youtube.com/user/yogawithadriene
❑ Yoga With Kassandra:
https://www.youtube.com/user/yogawithkassandra

At a later stage you could start your own Facebook fan page to keep in touch with your students and promote yourself (if that is what feels good to you).

More on personal branding? Check Chapter 7.6!

Nurture your "Public Relations"!

On Wikipedia I found the following definition of Public Relations:

Public relations (PR) is the practice of managing the spread of information between an individual or an organization and the public (...) The aim of public relations is to inform the public and ultimately persuade them to maintain a certain view about the organization, its leadership, products, or of political decisions. (...) Success in the field of public relations requires

46

a deep understanding of the interests and concerns of each of the client's many publics. The public relations professional must know how to effectively address those concerns using the most powerful tool of the public relations trade, which is publicity.

PR combines all activities that you use to present a positive image of yourself and/or your yoga studio on the one hand, and to steadily nurture the relationship with your audience on the other hand. PR activities include:

❑ **The press release** – The secret of a good press release is having an interesting story. A press release is sent to journalists with the aim of drawing attention for a current event or a certain viewpoint. The biggest advantage of writing and sending a press release - if your message has news value - is that the journalist in question will use your press release and make it a news story. This article will be picked up by the newspaper, news website, radio and/or TV, and is priceless advertisement for your studio. Subjects on which you can write a press release can be very diverse. A few examples:
  o You can send out a press release to the local newspaper of your city, village or community to announce the opening of your yoga studio.
  o There is news value in showing that yoga is on the rise - based on available information.
  o If you are planning on an exotic trip to work on your skills as a yoga teacher, this could also have a certain news value for the local media. This is also an opportunity to brand yourself.

Public Relations and writing press releases in particular, is a craft. As with every form of specialization, it is recommended to gather advice from professionals. If you want to experiment with writing and sending press releases, you should check out below book:

o "How To Write A Press Release" – by Brian Cook

On the below mentioned websites you can find tips & tricks on how to write an effective press release:
  o https://www.yogitimes.com/article/tips-yoga-business-pr-press-releases-campaigns-how-to-write
  o http://www.wikihow.com/Write-a-Press-Release
  o http://www.marketingdonut.co.uk/marketing/pr/writing-a-press-release/a-complete-guide-towriting-an-effective-press-release

❏ **Open house** – The aim of an open house event or open day is to let your students get to know you, your colleagues and your yoga studio. The open house event will also help maintain your public relations. You are able to invite a journalist of a local newspaper or radio station and get to speak to potential students at the same time. This allows you to answer any possible questions or remove concerns.

❏ **The workshop** – Did you invite a (internationally renowned) guest teacher for a unique workshop at your yoga studio? This will attract students and set yourself apart from other studios. This is also the moment to inform (local and/or specialized) press. A guest teacher specializing in pregnancy yoga might prove interesting to magazines that focus on (pregnant) women.

❏ **Public speaking** – If your an expert in your field, then you should talk to as many people as possible about what you do. Not only do you nurture your public relations this way, but you also help build a positive reputation and contribute to your personal branding.

❏ **Your relationship with your employees** – Keeping your employees informed of the performance of your yoga studio is a must. After all, they are the ambassadors of your studio and they help form the foundation for word-of-mouth advertisement. Besides, they are the first people to inform visitors of your yoga studio on products or services. You could send out a monthly "office" newsletter to all your employees, but it would be better to gather together at fixed moments in time - in an official way. A meeting will not only contribute to better internal communication, but also to a closer involvement of your employees. It is also a moment to discuss, giving each employee the space and time to share his or her opinion with the entire team.

❑ **Sponsorships** – Linking your (studio) name to a local organization, celebrity or event can contribute to building a reliable reputation. Is a yoga festival organized nearby? Ask if you can collaborate or propose to teach a class. Does your studio focus on runners or swimmers? Sponsor the local running or swimming association.

As you can see, PR goes a lot further than writing and sending out a press release. Nurturing your relations with you target audience goes through different channels, but they all contribute to a reliable and positive reputation. Besides, PR improves top-of-mind, which makes people think of you or your studio when they think of yoga. In other words, you will be seen as the expert in your field.

7.2. Your own website!

The role of Google in the growth of your yoga studio?

No matter how you look at it, the Internet can no longer be eliminated from our daily lives. Whether it is to book a hotel, order a pizza, search information on your next trip or to find a yoga studio in your area, Google always has the appropriate response. I say Google, but there are obviously other search engines that can help you find an answer to your question.

Before elaborating on the importance of Google to your yoga studio, I would like to ask you to put aside this book, start up Google and enter the following search criteria: Yoga + city where your studio is based (for example: yoga Ghent). Is your studio listed on the first page of the search results? Are you ranked first on the results page? If this is the case, congratulations, you are already well on your way and you have most like invested in a website or even in advertisements on the Google network (7.). If you are not listed or somewhere at the bottom of search results, there's room for improvement and room to let your yoga studio thrive.

As an example I'll use the search "Yoga Antwerpen" on Google.be

We can see 3 prominent parts on the Google search results page when looking for "Yoga Antwerpen".

1. A map of studios in Antwerp is displayed. This part of Google Maps is a very powerful tool as it immediately offers you a visual map of yoga studios in your area. If your studio doesn't appear on the map, people that are looking for a yoga studio in the area where you are based, unfortunately will not find your studio. Not to worry: Google offers a step-by-step instruction on how to add your yoga studio on Google Maps. Have a look at the help pages of Google: https://www.google.com/business/

2. We can also find the results of the people or companies that are willing to pay to appear first on the search results page when people enter a specific search (in our case "Yoga Antwerpen"). In other words, these people or companies advertise (against payment) using keywords that are relevant to their website and therefore relevant to their business. This form of paid advertisement is called Google AdWords. AdWords is an important part of the search giant Google.

"Google AdWords is an online advertising service developed by Google, where advertisers pay to display brief advertising copy, product listings, and video content within the Google ad network to web users. Google AdWords' system is based partly on cookies and partly on keywords determined by advertisers. Google uses these characteristics to place advertising copy on pages where they think it might be relevant. Advertisers pay when users divert their browsing to click on the advertising copy. Partner websites receive a portion of the generated income."
(source: https://en.wikipedia.org/wiki/AdWords).

Yoga Lessen & Meditatie
[Adv.] www.ayuryoga.be/Yoga-En-Meditatie ▾
In Groep Of Privé Yoga Lessen, Met Persoonlijke Begeleiding Vanaf 10€
Alleen of met 2 · Stress verminderen · Meer energie · Online Boeken Mogelijk
Prijzen · Massages · Yoga · Pijn Of Klachten

Ingeborg bij jou thuis | Schrijf in op Iedereen Yoga
[Adv.] www.iedereenyoga.com/ ▾
Yoga met Ingeborg bij jou thuis. Beschikbaar op pc, tablet, smartphone en tv!
6 lessenreeksen · Altijd beschikbaar · Begeleiding door Ingeborg · 210 minuten video
Een houding vinden · Go with the flow · In beweging zijn · Op adem komen · Energie opbouwen

3. Below the "paid" part you find the websites that Google finds relevant when using the search "Yoga Antwerpen". So, a good, organic (in other words, a **non-paid**) position on Google is an added value to your studio. Remember your own search behavior and what links you click on when visiting Google. Most of the time you don't go past the maps part, the paid part and the first organic search results on Google's first results page.

I would like to have my own website but I'm not sure where to start!

Just as teaching a yoga class is a specialism, building a website is also something that you could best leave to someone who knows what they're doing. 'Cobbler stick to your last, yogi stick to your mat' is very applicable in this context. You could obviously figure out how to build a website yourself, but it will cost you a lot of time and money. Remember all the hours and all the money you have invested in becoming a professional yoga teacher.

If you don't have a website yet, it is wise to have one made. Your own website will give you many advantages:

1. People can find your studio on the Internet, in other words your studio has an online business card where people can find the following information:
    a. Where your studio is located
    b. What the price per class is or which pricing

model you offer

    c. How to contact your studio (email, phone number)

    d. How your classes are organized

    e. Who the yoga teachers are

    f. The workshops you offer

    g. News on your studio

    h. Images, videos, impressions of your studio

    i. Etc.

2. If you have your own website than you can also promote it by means of paid advertisement on Google, Facebook, Youtube. More about this later!

3. Your own website sets your studio apart you from studios without a website and/or online presence. Wordpress (http://wordpress.org/) offers you the possibility to build your own website and blog also check out https://www.wix.com. You will need to hire someone for hosting and someone that can get your Wordpress website up and running. That someone is a website builder or an IT specialist with technical knowledge of Wordpress. Wix allows you do set up a website without the support of a developer.

   There are companies specialized in building websites. The cost of having your website built depends strongly on your demands and the company you work with. The more elaborate your demands are, the higher the price. Thus, you will have to pay for your logo and corporate identity separately, and the price will on the contractor you choose. For designing logos and websites, I work with www.99designs.com, but you can also contact design agencies or freelance designers.

My website is online, but I can't seem to find it in Google's search results!

Oh no!!! Your website is online, but when searching for it on Google, it doesn't appear in Google's search results.

Check: https://www.seomechanic.com/why-is-my-website-not-showing-in-google-search-results/

Google will answer this common question for you: https://support.google.com/webmasters/answer/35769?hl=en

It's also important to have the website designer build your website with this information in mind.

My website is online and can be found on Google, but I'm not ranked first!

Ranking first is important as most people only click on the first few results. It rarely happens that you click on a result that is found on the third page. Therefore it's important that your website is not only found on Google, but also "scores" well on Google. In other words: your website should appear as one of the first results when people are looking for your studio or for yoga in the vicinity of your studio. To score better on Google, we use Search Engine Marketing (SEM). Search Engine Marketing is the specialism that makes web pages findable for search engines. This means that a web page will have prominence in the search results when a user enters a relevant keyword for that website. Because the web page can be found more easily, it increases the effectiveness of advertisement on the Internet. Search Engine Marketing can be divided in two subcategories: Search Engine Optimization (SEO) and Search Engine Advertising (SEA) (source: Wikipedia).

Search Engine Optimization (SEO)

Search Engine Optimization (SEO) is the collective term for all techniques that one can adapt to ensure that a website scores well (in other words; achieving a better position on the search results page of Google without spending money on advertisement).

I think it's important to know that using SEO-techniques can influence your website's ranking on Google or any other search engine. It would take up too much time to explain all the different techniques. Besides, Google regularly changes the way they rank websites, which will make many techniques quickly outdated. Because of that, I prefer to refer you to https://moz.com/learn/seo; a comprehensive online guide to work on optimizing your website for search engines in order to rank better and attract more visitors (potential clients).

Google also helps users to rank better:
https://support.google.com/webmasters/answer/7451184?hl=en

http://static.googleusercontent.com/media/www.google.com/nl//webmasters/docs/search-engine-optimization-starter-guide.pdf

(can be a bit out-dated but it covers the fundamentals)

You'll quickly notice that SEO is a technical issue. Some tips are easily implemented, whereas other tips demand more technical knowledge. Depending on your expectations concerning your website, you can have an SEO-specialist advise you. Also, the way your website is built is half the work done. If you take Google's guidelines into consideration when beginning to build your website (https://support.google.com/webmasters/answer/35769?hl=en) , you're halfway there!

Search Engine Advertising (SEA)

Search Engine Advertising (SEA), Paid Search, PPC (pay-per-click) is a fee-required technique to rank higher or next to the organic (free) search results. The advertisement will be shown when a search engine user enters a word or a phrase that is linked to the advertisement. The advertiser only pays for the search engine user that clicks on one of his ads. The advertisement refers to the website of the advertiser. (Source: Wikipedia)

Again, I would also like to refer to the specialized literature and people/companies that are specialized in setting up and managing online advertisement through Google's advertisement-program "AdWords". These online Ads are an important source of income for Google, so Google is more than happy to help existing and prospective advertisers (such as yourself) to set up online Ad-campaigns on their network.

https://adwords.google.com/ you allows you to start creating and managing online advertisements. Using the tips that Google puts at your disposal http://static.googleusercontent.com/media/www.google.com/nl //adwords/pdf/hc/growing_adwords_en.pdf, you will already be one step closer to realizing an online advertisement campaign for your yoga studio. Again, I suggest finding help of experts on the matter so that you can achieve the optimal results, such as:

1. Generating as many views as possible (reach).
Some companies find it important to be top-of-mind. Therefore, their strategy might be to reach as many people as possible through Google AdWords. For a local company this strategy is not interesting, since you mainly want to reach people in the vicinity of your company, not from the entire country or world.

2. Attracting more visitors to your website.
This seems like the right goal at a first glance, since it will mean more visitors and more potential clients for you studio, but when taking a closer look, you could well end up

disappointed. We do want more visitors, but when you have a yoga studio in Antwerp do you really want to attract visitors from France, the Netherlands or Ghent? You're probably only interested in attracting visitors from the area. All in all your yoga studio is a local (small) business. It's crucial to only spend money on advertisements that will reach people from the area. Google wouldn't be Google if this weren't one of their main strengths (a USP, remember?). Google AdWords will allow you to only show advertisement to people that search with specific search items. The search item "yoga" will attract many visitors to your website, for example, but the search item "Yoga Antwerp" is much more important for you, since it will attract people that are consciously looking for yoga in Antwerp.

3. Getting as many conversions as possible.
More important than reaching the number of visitors, is knowing and measuring which actions these visitors have performed. Your goal can be to have visitors contact you via a contact form on your website, or to have visitors call your studio with their questions, or to have visitors purchase something through your website. These 3 examples are illustrations of possible conversions. In other words; your visitors will take certain actions after visiting your website which will increase the purchase intent.

As indicated before, I think it's more important to introduce you to the possibilities of advertisement with Google, than to give you an entire course on how to get started.

If you do want to explore this matter, than I would like to refer you to Google and search for "ppc for beginners".

I also can recommend the following book:
   ❑ "Google AdWords for Dummies" - by Howie Jacobson

7.3. Expand your online presence and reputation
In the last chapter, we have elaborately discussed how to make strategic use of the worlds' most important search

engine, Google, to attract students on the one hand and to promote yourself by having your own website on the other hand.

Making yourself visible in Google for your present and future students by means of a website about you and your studio is a first step in making use of the opportunities that internet has to offer with respect to promotion and marketing.

Below, you will find an overview of other online activities you can undertake to make you and/or your studio more visible on the Internet on the one hand and to promote yourself and/or your studio online on the other hand.

Facebook

Next to Google, Facebook maybe the most important online service on which you can promote yourself and/or your studio. Facebook, like Google, offers a big advantage. They are perfectly aware of the interests of their users and they offer companies the possibility to select their target group based on age, language, gender, interests, and region. Such powerful restrictions are invaluable to companies when it comes to defining a target group. The (advertisement) message targets people who are most likely interested in your offer. I use the words 'most likely', because it cannot be completely ruled out that someone is not interested in your offer. You are not necessarily interested in everything that has to do with yoga just because you have indicated to be interested in yoga. Facebook does however permit you to further restrict your target group, increasing the possibility that the people within this selective group are interested in your offer.

Besides the possibility to select your target group, there are other reasons why you should create a Facebook page:

1. Millions of people within your target group have a personal profile page on the social network site Facebook.com

2. As a business owner, surely you want to promote your business where your current and future customers can be found.

3. Your Facebook page is comparable to a big neon sign on the busiest crossroad of your town or community. The only exception is that it is free of charge. Your customers and their friends can be found on Facebook, and you have the opportunity to tell a whole lot more on your Facebook page than in an advertisement.

Think of your Facebook Page as an extension of your business. It is an easy way to share relevant information (such as articles or events) and to stay top-of-mind with your target audience. To maximise the impact of your Facebook page, you should mention your Facebook address Facebook.com/yourstudio on your business cards, website and other marketing materials. Before advertising on Facebook, you should create a Facebook (company-, product-, service-, brand-) page.

Below you will find a short roadmap to start promoting yourself or your yoga studio on Facebook.

1. Surf to https://www.facebook.com/pages/create and follow the steps.
2. Invite your current students (for example in a newsletter or through oral communication after your yoga class), your Facebook friends/acquaintances and business contacts (fellow teachers, suppliers) to *like* your page.
3. Bring your business to life by responding to the interests of your target group with 'unique' *content*. By *content* we mean articles, pictures, quotes, personal anecdotes, coverage of workshops, events, etc.
4. Reach more people by sending the right message to the right people. You can do this by starting an ad campaign on: https://www.facebook.com/ads/create/.

Increasing the reach of your Facebook page can be done through different on- and offline channels. Your current students and employees can become online ambassadors and refer friends and acquaintances to your page.

Do you want to know more about how to promote yourself (personal branding) or your yoga studio on Facebook? Check below (reading) tips:

- ❑ Facebook marketing for dummies – by John Haydon
- ❑ The official Facebook page on Facebook marketing: https://www.facebook.com/marketing

Foursquare

Foursquare is a free app that helps you and your friends make the most of where you are.

Foursquare is perfect for local marketing. I use the app to discover interesting sites in new cities I visit. Interesting sites tend to have a good review score and a lot of check-ins. You can easily search for a yoga studio in city X. If your studio is not listed in the results you are missing out on an opportunity to attract new students. If you open the Foursquare app (https://foursquare.com/download), you are able to search for a yoga studio in the area where you are situated or the area you will travel to. For the sake of convenience, I search for a yoga studio in Ghent (my hometown) and get the following result:

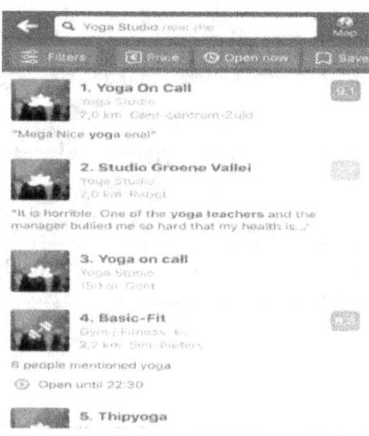

What is also noticeable is that these results all have the same logo (lotus flower). This is because the owners of the specific yoga studios have not yet claimed their studio. I recommend owners of a yoga studio to claim your studio on Foursquare so you can help define the content of your page on Foursquare.

Surf to https://foursquare.com/venue/claim and follow the steps.
Once you have officially claimed your studio and it is registered to your name, you can start promoting your studio.

1. Add pictures
Adding pictures will make your page more attractive and it offers prospective students more information before visiting your studio. People are more likely to visit a place they have already seen then to take a leap of faith.

2. Add extra information
A description of your yoga studio and extra information such as phone number, web address and Facebook page are examples of relevant information you can add to your "venue page". Knowing when your studio is open, if you can pay by card and if you have WiFi, is crucial information for new students.

3. Add tips
Tips can help prospective students choose your studio or enhance their experience with your studio. Do you offer unique classes or drinks? Let them know by adding tips!

Next to making your venue page appealing by providing detailed information and visuals, you can choose to - just like Facebook and Google - show paid ads to Foursquare users who are looking for a yoga studio near you. These ads will make your studio stand out from the other studios that are listed on Foursquare's result page. This will result in more customers for your studio!

Find more information on the advertisement programme on
http://business.foursquare.com/ads/ &
http://business.foursquare.com/.

More tips on how to promote your yoga studio on Foursquare
you can find on
http://www.socialmediaexaminer.com/foursquare-marketing-
tips.

If you want to learn more you can check out below book
recommendations.
- ❏ "Social Location Marketing Outshining Your
    Competitors on Foursquare,
- ❏ Gowalla, Yelp & Other Location Sharing Sites"– by
    Simon Salt;
    *Even though Gowalla no longer exists, the book
    remains an important reference book that explains the
    principles of location based marketing (LMB)*
- ❏ "The Power of Foursquare" – by Carmine Gallo

Twitter
Opinions on Twitter are divided. Although there are books
written (see below) on how to market yourself and your
business on Twitter, Twitter mostly remains a niche social
networking site.Twitter can especially be interesting if you are
a (international) yoga teacher who lives off the recognition of
the yoga community (e.g. Tara Stiles
https://twitter.com/TaraStiles or
Kino MacGregor https://twitter.com/kinomacgregor).

Do you like to spontaneously and regularly share an - for your
target audience - interesting tweet (a short message) without
having the stress of having to tweet every single day AND do
you like interacting with your followers (people who follow your
tweets on Twitter), then Twitter might be for you. You definitely
shouldn't start using Twitter because it sounds popular. Try to
be honest and ask yourself whether you really feel like
tweeting.

Twitter does offer various possibilities to promote yourself or your studio:

1. Tweeps, people on Twitter, ask their network (followers) for purchase advice. A simple search allows you to see who is looking for yoga in your area
2. Tweeps share their location with their followers. They don't only share their location with followers on Twitter, but also with their friends on Facebook and Foursquare.
3. If you have your own Twitter account, you are able to start following people. The Twitter Advcanced Search (https://twitter.com/search-advanced) allows you to search for tweeps who have used the word "yoga" in a tweet, who write Dutch and who live in the vicinity of your studio. You are able to follow these people and get in touch with them.
4. Use Twitter as a newsfeed to stay informed about current global events that have your interest. As a yogi, you might be interested in news about yoga. Twitter allows you to easily stay informed about a particular subject by creating lists (https://support.twitter.com/articles/76460-how-to-use-twitter-lists). You can for example make a list of your students who are on Twitter or a list of yoga news websites. This way, you can structure your Twitter account *and* have an easy overview of your fields of interest.

Some suggestions of yoga tweeps or yoga-related twitter accounts to follow:
- https://twitter.com/itsallyoga_baby
- https://twitter.com/kathrynbudig
- https://twitter.com/TaraStiles
- https://twitter.com/yogabear
- https://twitter.com/Yoga_Journal
- https://twitter.com/kinomacgregor
- https://twitter.com/yogadork
- https://twitter.com/gaiam

- https://twitter.com/MindBodyGreen
- https://twitter.com/elephantjournal
- https://twitter.com/yogitimesonline

5. Do you have competitors or colleagues on Twitter? Follow them as it allows you to stay informed of their doings. As Twitter is a niche market in Belgium (less so in the Netherlands), you will not find many Belgian yoga studios on Twitter. In the Netherlands, they are one step ahead and a healthy competition exists, both on- and offline. Be careful not to spam your followers telling people to come to your studio. Nobody is interested in that. In other words, Twitter is a tool to connect with likeminded people online and to interact with these people by sharing relevant - to your target audience - information. Twitter is not the right channel to constantly inform people they have to buy something from you.

Do you want to know more about how to use Twitter to promote yourself and/or your yoga studio? Then definitely check these book recommendations:
- "Twitter Marketing For Dummies" – by Kyle Lacy
- "Twitter Marketing An Hour a Day" – by Hollis Thomases
- "Twitter Power 2.0 How to Dominate Your Market One Tweet at a Time"– by Joel Comm

Google Places
Register your company for Google Places
http://www.google.be/business/placesforbusiness ;
https://support.google.com/plus/answer/1713911?hl=en)   is always a good idea and completely free of charge! Google Places is a Google service that allow you to be listed on Google Maps so that your (future) clients are able to easily find you. Business owners that have been registered can manage the information concerning the physical location (pictures, opening hours, customer reviews, etc.) of their company. This means that when a prospective client searches

for a product or service that you offer, your company will be listed in the organic (non-paying) results, as well as on a Google Map.

If we look at Google Places in more detail, we find a list of yoga studios in Antwerp with their address, website and a pointer. These pointers can be found on the map that Google shows on the right side of your page. You can see where each studio is located in one glance.

We also see a link to Google reviews. These are customer reviews. These reviews are very valuable to your yoga studio, as you receive immediate feedback on how students rate your studio. People (prospective customers) looking for a yoga studio will be influenced by the reviews of other students. Google reviews can be considered word of mouth advertising for your studio. People tend to be influenced by them so it is recommended to do well and respond to dissatisfied students who leave a bad review. Google lets you respond to reviews of customers on your review page, which will only improve your reputation.

In short: get your business on Google Places (https://www.google.com/business/)

YouTube

YouTube, the world's largest collection of videos on the internet and owned by Internet behemoth Google offers another way to bring yourself and your yoga studio to the attention of (prospective) students. Just as millions of people use Google every single day, you will also find millions of people on YouTube. Millions of people - including your future students.

Did you ever notice that when you look for something on Google, you will often find YouTube videos among the highest ranking results? Google does this, as these videos can be extremely relevant as a result of a particular search. The following example shows how Google lists several YouTube videos after my search for "vinyasa yoga beginners".

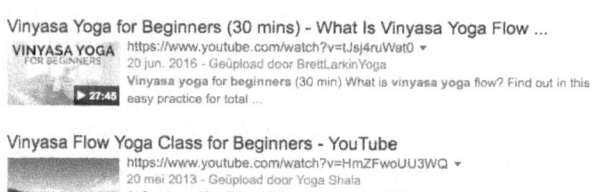

If you want to promote yourself or your yoga studio on YouTube with the purpose of making yourself more noticeable in the search results when people are looking for a product or service that you offer, I recommend creating a YouTube Channel. Watch how this is done on, of course, YouTube: https://www.youtube.com/watch?v=b38ef8n1p4U.

Once your channel is up & running, you can add videos.

Here are some tips:
- ❑ Upload relevant videos - in other words: make a video in which you introduce your yoga studio or make videos in which you teach a yoga class.
- ❑ Give your video a fitting title, a title that describes what the video is about. This avoids a video titled "DC005.mp4", in which you introduce your studio, from

being excluded in the Google search results if someone Googles your yogastudio name. In our example, the title can be something like this:

"Yoga-On-Call, a tour of our yoga studio in Ghent". The most important keywords in this title are "yoga-on-call", "yoga studio", "Ghent". By including relevant keywords in your title, the keywords that are being used by prospective students in their searches, you will increase your chance of being listed if someone is looking for "yoga studio Ghent" or "yoga Ghent". As we now know, it is important to claim the highest-ranking results in the results page, as these are the results that get the best click-through rates.

❑ Once you have uploaded videos, you are able to share these on your Google Places page, your Foursquare venue page, your Facebook page, etc. The expression "sharing is caring" applies here. The more you share relevant information with your (prospective) target audience and the more this audience notices you and finds this information relevant, the bigger the chance that this target audience shares your information with their network.

I have limited myself to the bare essentials of YouTube marketing. If you desire more tips & tricks I recommend reading the following:

❑ "YouTube Marketing Power" – by Jason Miles
❑ "YouTube for Business" – by Michael Miller

Spotify

Spotify is a digital music streaming service that gives you access to millions of songs. You do not buy these songs, but instead pay a monthly fee to Spotify and get unlimited usage on smartphone, tablet or computer. In addition to the millions of songs, Spotify offers the possibility to create and share playlists. The advantages of these playlists include being able to name the list, adding selected songs to the list and other Spotify users being able to subscribe to your playlist. My search "vinyasa" yielded the following result:

Nothing brings people closer together than music. Chances are that the people belonging to your target audience share the same taste in music. Yoga is perfect for bringing people together by letting them create a playlist based on a specific theme such as vinyasa yoga, or asking their opinion about music that was played during your yoga class. Remember to share your actions on Spotify with your friends, acquaintances and students on all the social networks in which you are active.

You can promote yourself or your studio by creating playlists of your favourite yoga music or the music you use in class. As a first step, you can let your students know that they can subscribe to your playlists (I definitely would, because I always wonder which music is caressing my ears during an intense yoga class). Students who subscribe to your playlist(s) automatically share it with their friends and acquaintances on Spotify. In short: extra exposure for your studio and the possibility to differentiate from your competitors.

Here is a gift from me to you… A playlist with my favorite "yoga" music:
https://goo.gl/7SBeps

Do you want to know what Spotify can mean for you and your studio? Check the following tips:

- ❑ "Spotify For Dummies" – by Kim Gilmour
- ❑ "Sams Teach Yourself Spotify in 10 Minutes" – by Michael Miller

Instagram

Instagram, a free mobile app to share digital photos or videos, falls into the category of visual marketing. Images strike a chord with consumers (simply think of how you select a bottle of wine in the supermarket). Especially on social networks, pictures tend to get more engagement than a simple written update. Brands or companies who post pictures on their Facebook page, increase the interaction with their community by 39% (source: http://mashable.com/2012/09/28/marketers-facebook-wrong).

With more than 800 million active users, Instagram has become a big player in social networking. This also explains why Facebook, the king of social networking sites, has bought Instagram in 2012 for 1 billion dollars
(source: http://abcnews.go.com/blogs/technology/2012/04/facebook-buys-instagram-for-1-billion).

Like with any online service, you'll do well to familiarise yourself with the service before starting to market yourself or your studio through that particular service. It is recommended that you first try out Instagram yourself and observe what other people or famous brands do. Once you are familiar with the filters, hashtags and likes, you can start using Instagram to support your personal branding and brandawareness.

Keep in mind the following:

- If you already have a Twitter account, it is smart to register the same name for Instagram. When photos or videos are shared on Twitter, the @username will link to your Twitter bio.
- Think carefully about what you want to accomplish when sharing photos and videos on Instagram. As with

other networking sites, it is important to share relevant images with your followers instead of posting one advertisement after the other.

- Use hashtags (http://nl.wikipedia.org/wiki/Hashtag). These hashtags (for example #yoga or #asanas) allow users to easily find certain content.

Instagram is working hard to support companies with the marketing of their business through its service. You can stay informed of the latest news, tips & tricks by reading their blog http://business.instagram.com/blog/.

Some suggested reading on Instagram marketing and visual marketing that I would like to share with you:

- ❑ " Instagram Marketing (2018): The Guide Book for Using Photos on Instagram to Gain Millions of Followers Quickly and to Skyrocket your Business (Influencer and Social Media Marketing)" - David J Green

Newsletter

We can be brief about email marketing. An absolute must for every yoga studio! Emailing your customers is the minimum you can do to inform them of everything that goes on in your studio. Moreover, you will make sure to create that top-of-mind awareness for yourself/yoga/your yogastudio. The icing on the cake has to be that this form of (direct) marketing is (nearly) for free. You can gather the email addresses of your students for free and sending a simple email does not have to cost any money.

Over the years, email marketing has been given a negative connotation as people received tons of emails of each and every company where they are or once were customers, without having explicitly asked for this. This form of unsolicited communications (spam) is absolutely not appreciated. It is therefore important that you ask your (new) students for permission to occasionally send them an email with information about your studio, workshops, etc.

The simplest form of email marketing is gathering email addresses of your students and emailing them relevant information on a regular basis. However, if you send your students emails using your own email account, you do not have insight into the number of people having opened your email or having clicked on which link. This is valuable information, so it is recommended to work with an email marketing service provider. Such a provider enables you to design your emails (to match to your company brand), organise your email addresses, schedule and send your emails, and last but not least, to analyse all actions. After all, it is good to know if your effort is paying off!

Let me illustrate this by giving an example. Yoga studio X sends a newsletter to its students every month. The owner spends a whole day writing the content (articles, workshops, etc), the layout of the newsletter and updating the website with the information in the newsletter. The owner devotedly sends the newsletter, knowing she does something good for her studio. She does not know who actually read the newsletter, who clicked on the links to the website and who registered for a specific workshop after reading the newsletter. In short, she does not know how effective the newsletter actually is and whether spending all day writing it is worth the effort. She has possibly spent all day working on a newsletter that only 5 students have actually read. In order to know how effective your email marketing is, you are advised to use an email marketing service provider.

An overview of popular email marketing service providers:
- ❑ Mailchimp (This is the one I use and am satisfied with) – Completely free, so check http://eepurl.com/MOkiL
- ❑ Namastelight (genious name and genious marketing when aiming at yoga studios) http://www.namastelight.com/
- ❑ YourMailingListProvider - http://www.ymlp.com/nl/
- ❑ Constant Contact - http://www.constantcontact.com/

Please note that I don't have experience with all the aforementioned email marketing service providers. From my own experience, I can state that Mailchimp (http://eepurl.com/MOkiL) is absolutely great, but I also know yoga studio owners who recommend Namastelight, YourMailingListProvider and Constant Contact. Most providers have an overview of features on their website so that you can easily compare and decide which one will best suit your needs. Internet offers many reviews and these can also aid in your search for the ideal email marketing service provider.

Here is an overview of the pros and cons of email marketing:

❑ Advantages:

- o **Cost**
  In comparison to other marketing methods, the cost of email marketing is relatively low.

- o **Increased revenues**
  It only takes 1 newsletter to reach all your active and inactive students and (re)create interest for your studio. Even though there is no way of knowing how much your revenues will increase by sending newsletters, it is safe to say that your mailing will at least generate some revenue.

- o **Tracking**
  Email marketing allows you to track the effectiveness of your efforts. The effectiveness of email marketing comprises:
  - Knowing who received your newsletter and who did not. Reasons for not receiving your newsletter (even if registered) are: a faulty email address, an inactive email address or closed account, or the newsletter is delivered to the spam folder.

- Knowing who not only received your newsletter, but who also opened or read your email. More importantly than knowing who received your newsletter is knowing whose interest in you/your studio is actually enough to take the time and effort to open and read your email.
- Knowing who clicked on what link. Receiving, opening and reading are the 3 basic elements of an effective email campaign. As a 4th element, we can add that knowing who clicked on what link in your newsletter makes it a successful email campaign.

- **Quick**
  Email marketing can be quickly executed and generates fast results.

□ Disadvantages:

- **Easy to ignore**
  You are definitely not the only one who has discovered the power of email marketing. There is a large probability that the people who receive your email receive several newsletters on a daily basis. Moreover, it is impossible to know whether all the people who have subscribed to your newsletter are still interested in yoga and/or your studio. Email is very easy to ignore, and as a result you may not reach all the people you would like to. That is why it is so crucial in your email marketing strategy to track the open and click-through rates of your emails.

- **Spammy**
  Consequently, your emails may be perceived as spam and can therefore be ignored. Remember to only send mail when you have something

"valuable" to say. Also keep in mind the following tips for an effective email campaign.

7 tips for an effective email campaign:

1. Keep it short

True, you're sending a newsletter because you have exciting and relevant information to share with your students, but you don't necessarily have to share all this information in your email. If you find it difficult to reduce the information, you might want to use a table of contents at the beginning of your email. This way, people will see all the items you have incorporated into your newsletter and are able to click on the subject of their interest. I also recommend working with bullet points. They provide more structure than long sentences and increase the readability of your newsletter. My absolute preference goes to including a summary of your stories in the newsletter and providing a link to the complete story on your website (blog).

2. The subject line of your newsletter makes a difference

The title or subject line of your newsletter is usually the first thing your students will see. In other words, the subject will determine whether students will open and read your newsletter.

Subject lines such as "monthly newsletter" or "here we are again" usually reveal little about the content and can therefore be easily ignored. The subject lines are not appealing enough to trigger your students. You will always be able to reach the faithful reader (student), but the passive student that visits you once a month will be more likely to ignore your newsletter when the subject line does not arouse their interest. A newsletter with the subject line "Register for our unique workshop with X" of "Registration yoga weekend" or "Welcome new teacher Z", or a combination of subjects such as "unique yoga workshop with X – register for the yoga weekend – welcome Y" can therefore mean the difference between a recipient opening your newsletter or not.

A general guideline is using the topic that you think most students will be interested in. The subject line is suitable for testing what works for your target audience and what doesn't. They might like simple and straightforward or a touch of humor. You won't know until you put it to the test.

3. To measure is to know
Just as important as sending a newsletter is analyzing the results (see effectiveness). You might wonder how beneficial it is to analyze reports of previous newsletters, but it helps to draw up future newsletters. Which subjects are read or clicked on the most? On which day did most students open your newsletter? For instance, a newsletter that is sent on Saturday is less likely to be read than a newsletter that is sent on Tuesday (http://kb.mailchimp.com/article/when-is-the-best-time-to-send-emails). Which students always open your newsletter and which don't? Is there any connection to the frequency with which they visit your studio? Analyzing reports adds to the success of your (future) campaigns.

4. Get social
Is your studio active on Facebook, Twitter or other social media sites? Motivate your readers to follow you or become a fan of your page, if only to promote your Facebook page or to encourage your readers to share your stories with their friends and acquaintances. It is also a good idea to share your newsletters with your fans or followers on social media sites. This way, you will encourage your followers (who have not yet registered) to subscribe to your newsletter.

5. Be relevant and interesting
Make sure that your emails are interesting and not just another advertising message. You can certainly encourage your readers to attend a workshop or inform them about a new membership structure, but first make sure that your newsletter is interesting to read. Ask yourself what you like to read, which newsletters appeal to you and why.

6. Give your readers the option to unsubscribe
Nothing is more annoying than to receive newsletters from companies that you not wish to receive, because what these

companies have to offer you no longer excites you. This also applies to your yoga studio. There will undoubtedly be students in your mailing list who are no longer interested in yoga and/or your studio. You would do well -and it is required by law- to add an unsubscribe link to your newsletter. Tip: place this (not too flashy) link at the very bottom of your email, so you don't accidentally encourage people to unsubscribe.

7. Look & Feel

If your newsletter is not visually appealing, chances are slim that your audience will have a fascinating read. Your newsletter should have a design that is appealing enough to continue reading. The design of your newsletter should be consistent with the look & feel of your website or even your entire branding (see 7.1 Branding your yoga studio)

Do you want more tips & tricks or deepen your knowledge on above tips? Check the following online articles:

❑ "Top 10 Tips for Great Newsletters"
https://www.mdirector.com/en/email-marketing-en/10-tips-for-creating-great-newsletters.html
❑ "7 Golden Steps to Creating an Effective Email Newsletter"
https://www.verticalresponse.com/blog/7-golden-steps-to-creating-an-effective-email-newsletter/

There are innumerable books about email marketing, but I recommend the following if you want to further your knowledge:
❑ "e-Mail Marketing For Dummies" – by John Arnold
❑ "The Rebel's Guide To Email Marketing" – by Jason Falls

Discount websites

The hype around discount website Groupon may be over, but discount websites have not ceased to exist. As long as there are people, there will be discounts. Who does not like a good discount? These discount websites offer the opportunity to promote your yoga studio. The biggest advantage of having an offer on a discount website is that you will undoubtedly attract new students. And that is ultimately what marketing is about.

Some advantages of discount websites at a glance:

1. Discount websites have a local focus

Your studio is located in a city or town and the majority of your students will live in the vicinity of your studio. A local focus in your marketing activities is advisable in order to let your studio grow. Discount websites fit perfectly into this local marketing focus, as they operate at city level and the visitors of these websites specify for which region they wish to receive discounts. In short, your offer will be shown only to those visitors who have indicated to be interested in deals in your area.

2. Discount websites send newsletters

Visitors register for a discount website and specify the region or city for which they would like to receive discounts. In addition, the discount websites send out newsletters to their registered visitors. Email marketing and of course attractive discounts keep the discount websites up and running. Even if the visitor doesn't have an interest in yoga (yet) or has never considered taking a yoga class, he/she will still receive an email with your promotional offer. This way, you are able to reach people you would otherwise never be able to reach.

3. The success rate of your offer or special deal is easily calculated

Placing a promotional offer on a discount website costs money. The good thing is that you can calculate how much money your promotion will cost, as you pay per visitor that accepts your offer. After purchasing your deal, the discount website sends them a confirmation email that they can show you when coming to class.
You could work out a special marketing program for these new students by recording their most important data (name, age,

(email) address, etc.) on a sheet (you can also use specialised CRM software or Excel – more about this later). This allows you to send the students an email with a promotion to purchase a monthly, quarterly or yearly subscription. This partially determines the success of your promotional offer. This offer is designed to attract new students, but it is completely up to you to convert these one-time visitors into loyal customers!

4. Discount websites are easily accessible

As an entrepreneur, you do not always have the time (and the money) to develop large marketing campaigns. For that reason, discount websites are very suitable for small businesses. They don't require hours of work and you pay for success. At first glance, the discount websites look like THE way to attract new students and to make your studio grow, but there is a downside to every upside:

- **Attracting disloyal customers**
  People who make use of discount websites are usually price-sensitive people or bargain hunters. Chances are that when there is no promotional discount, these people will stay away. The investment you have made to attract these people will vanish. Ultimately, you will have to look for customers who come regularly and are loyal to your studio.

- **Cannibalising your current customer base**
  There is a possibility that current, loyal students are active on a discount website where you have just launched a promotional offer or that these loyal students get wind of this deal. There is a danger that they, who always pay full price, will sign up for the promotional offer. You will not attract new students (the goal of your campaign) and you will also lose revenue (because these students would otherwise have paid full price). Please consider that loyal students may nevertheless be happy with this offer, thus adding to a greater (if possible) customer satisfaction among your

loyal students.

- **Attracting too many people**
Imagine that your campaign is so successful that hundreds of people register for one of your yoga classes at a significant discount. This may lead to some practical problems. Is your classroom big enough? Is there enough parking space?

- **The negative perception of discounts**
A discount on a can of vegetable soup may be a sweet deal. A discount on a yoga class may raise questions as to how well your studio is doing. Every promotional offer could lead to an undervaluation of your services. In other words: every promotional offer influences the perception of people.

Now that we have listed the pros and cons, discount websites could be a worthwhile opportunity to explore. Keep in mind that such a campaign is designed to attract new students and that you ought to have a follow-up plan once these new students have visited your studio.

I found an interesting article on Yoga Journal about the use of online coupons and yoga classes that I would like to share with you: https://www.yogajournal.com/teach/yoga-studio-groupon-coupons-new-students

Blog
When you are actively marketing yourself or your studio on the Internet, it could be a nice addition to start a blog (on your website or on, for example, www.medium.com), posting relevant articles for your target audience. Blogging, an important form of content marketing, will help being found on search engines and it will also benefit the interaction with your target audience, activating them to participate in the (online) conversation. Your blogs lend themselves to be shared on social media, such as Facebook or Twitter. This way, you will have unique content that you can share with your target

audience and that your target audience is able to share with their connections. Your message will be spread and you are building your online reputation as well as your brand.

Before you start blogging like mad, I would like you to consider the pros and cons.

The biggest advantage of blogging is that it is very easy to start. You only need to start writing and sharing your views with the world/your target audience. Making a blog is relatively easy. In Chapter 7.2 we already discussed Wordpress & Wix: a free software package to build website and blogs.

Other advantages are e.g.:
- A blog gives people a **reason to visit your website**. A blog gives you the possibility to let your voice be heard and create a more dynamic website.
- Blogging can contribute to creating a **sense of community**. By blogging about subjects that interest your target audience and inviting them to give their opinion, you can generate a sense of community.
- Google loves **unique and personal content**. In your blog you can share ideas, personal experiences, a movie or photo with your local community or the world. An article on AcroYoga in Antwerp will attract people from Antwerp to your site that were looking for AcroYoga in Antwerp on Google or another search engine. At the same time it is an opportunity to attract new students.

The biggest disadvantage of blogging is that it is **extremely time-consuming**. Although it is easy to start a blog, it takes a lot of time and effort to maintain the blog and keep it relevant. There is no use in starting a blog if you don't like writing or have little inspiration. Blogging regularly is a must to continue to appeal to people and your target audience.

Can't wait to start blogging? Have a look at below book suggestions that are divided into 3 categories:

1. Content marketing books:
   - ❏ "Epic Content Marketing" – by Joe Pulizzi
   - ❏ "Content Marketing For Dummies" – by Susan Gunelius

2. Books on Wordpress:
   - ❏ "WordPress All-in-One For Dummies" – by Lisa Sabin-Wilson

3. Books on blogging:
   - ❏ "Blogging All-in-One For Dummies" – by Susan Gunelius
   - ❏ "Blog, Inc." – by Joy Deangdeelert Cho

Miscellaneous
It goes without saying that there are other online possibilities to create awareness for yourself and your studio. It would take too much time to elaborate on all the possibilities (Tumblr, Pinterest, Medium...) and I have therefore decided to give you an insight into the most popular options. I don't rule out the possibility of discussing other online channels during my marketing workshops. Internet changes rapidly and that what isn't mainstream today, may just become that tomorrow.

Your experience and feedback are therefore very important to me. If you have a positive experience with a channel that hasn't been discussed in this book, I encourage you to share this with me. You can contact me with your experiences (mathieuvansteenberge@gmail.com or
https://www.facebook.com/mathieu.van.steenberge). I might update this book with your experience or send your tip(s) to the people who have subscribed to my newsletter. Sharing is caring, remember: ;-)

7.4. Expanding your presence and reputation in the analog world
The Internet plays an important role in building your reputation

and in contributing to the growth of your business. In addition to the world of Internet, there is the analog-, or offline world. Whether you like it or not, this analog world is where all the magic has to happen. If there is no offline monitoring of your online activities, then all your efforts will have been in vain. Moreover, the offline world provides numerous marketing possibilities to brand yourself and/or your studio, to attract more yoga students, to activate these students to come more often and thus to make more money. I'll discuss how that is done in this chapter.

Flyers

Everybody receives a flyer once in a while. Many people, including politicians, but also event managers and companies distribute flyers to promote themselves, their products or services. Flyers are perfect for spreading a message, promoting a product or service or a special offer. Printing flyers can be done in every color of the rainbow; there are big flyers, small flyers, and double-sided flyers. In short: you can find them in all available sizes. There are both advantages and disadvantages to using flyers.

❑ **Advantages:**

1. **Easy to produce**
   Designing, printing and distributing flyers is relatively easy.
2. **Easy to read**
   Due to the limited size of the flyer, the information is summarized and can be read in one glance.
3. **Cheap**
   In comparison to other promotional channels, the distribution of flyers is cheap. You can mail the flyers, hire a student, or invite your friends and family to help you distribute the flyers.

❑ **Disadvantages:**

1. **Easy to ignore**
   Because flyers are an accessible promotional tool, you aren't the only one spreading flyers. It is also easy to ignore when your flyer doesn't end up with the right people (read: your target audience). The impact of a flyer can be low in comparison to other promotional activities.

2. **Too short of a message**
   Because of its small size, the length of your message is limited. Getting to the point is necessary in order to attract the attention of the person who receives the flyer.

3. **No-advertising sticker on mailbox**
   Nowadays, many people have a sticker on their mailbox, indicating that they do not wish to receive unaddressed advertising. It is forbidden by law to ignore this sticker. Because of this, you are not able to reach all the people you would like to.

Some ideas to increase the impact of your flyer:

1. **Announce a special discount promotion or workshop**
   In order to maximise the impact, it is good practice to print an attractive promotion or workshop on your flyer. This way, you will give people a reason to pay attention to your flyer and to take action (registering for the workshop, asking for information, surfing to your website)

2. **Door-to-door distribution in the area surrounding your studio**
   a. *Paying:*
      If your time is valuable and you would like to invest in letting your village or town know that

you exist, then you could make use of the postal distribution service. More information can be found on the postal services' websites.

b. *Non-paying*
   Get your friends, family or enthusiastic/loyal students to distribute your flyers in the area surrounding your studio. You could, for instance, give a free class in return.

3. **Invest in an attractive and professional design**
   Appearances do matter. A visually attractive flyer will be noticed more quickly and increases your chance to get your message across.

4. **Mention your website**
   If you have a website, I suggest mentioning it on your flyer. This way, people can visit your website to get more information.

5. **Distribute your flyers in stores that your (potential) customers frequent**
   In order to maximize the impact, it is essential your message end up with the targeted audience. Distributing flyers in a store where they sell yoga wear could be a way to appeal to the right audience and increase your impact.

Posters

Posters are a good way to complement your flyers. If you're running a promotional campaign or if you want to inform people about a workshop, it makes sense to put up posters in relevant places, in addition to distributing flyers. These places could be local shops, restaurants or cafes. It is important that you look for places that your potential customers visit. Blogging, an important form of content marketing, will help being found on search engines and it will also benefit the interaction with your target audience, activating them to participate in the (online) conversation. All in all, it is your goal to generate more income by making marketing investments. The most important advantage of posters is that these - like flyers - offer a cheap and accessible way to spread your message. The biggest disadvantage is that it is too noncommittal. People see your poster and instantly decide whether to read it carefully or not. In this case, you would also want to look for places that your target audience frequents to have as much of an impact as possible. Please consider that no advertising tool is completely effective on its own and using a combination of promotional tools will maximize the impact.

Brochure

If you want to give more information to your current and future students, then you might want to consider creating a brochure. A brochure offers you more room and freedom to introduce yourself, your studio and your planned workshops. You have complete control over what you wish to share and to whom you want to give the brochure. You can also determine the size of the brochure, the thickness of the paper and the number of pages, so it will fit within your budget.

The disadvantage is that a brochure doesn't lend itself well to communicate with a wide audience as the price (of printing and distribution) will rise. Another disadvantage is that the moment the information regarding your studio changes, a brochure becomes outdated and therefore useless.

Calendar

How cool would it be to have your own personal yoga calendar each year? Not a boring calendar that you get for free when shopping at a department store, but a calendar you make yourself. For each month, you can choose a student or teacher performing his or her favorite asana. This allows you to give your studio a face and students feel more involved with and interested in your activities, which in turn leads to an increase in customer loyalty. Such a calendar also makes a great promotional gift or an opportunity to organise an end-of-year activity where you could give a personalized calendar to every student who gets a membership for say, 2 months minimum. This promotional offer can be mentioned on your website, in your newsletter and brought to the attention by distributing flyers and posters (in your studio as well as outside your studio). If we develop this idea a bit further, it could also be an opportunity to earn some extra money, in addition to your yoga classes. You can sell the calendar in your studio, on your website or during workshops.

Birthday Card
A small gesture but a world of difference it makes to send your students a personal birthday card. Don't we all like receiving cards of people that wouldn't necessarily remember your birthday? Moreover, writing cards is a warm and personal gesture (especially in times where most birthday wishes are posted on Facebook)

A birthday card has numerous advantages:
- You appeal to the hearts of your students, which makes them happy. Chances are that your birthday students will share this experience with his/her friends and acquaintances (word-of-mouth marketing).

- It is possible that your student hasn't visited your classes for a while or is going to another yoga studio. A personal birthday card allows your studio to get back on his or her radar. You're working on reactivating 'dormant' customers (more on this later).

- This gesture can set you apart from your competitors (that do not send a birthday card). In a competitive market it's the small gestures that can make a huge difference.

Some tips on how to develop this idea:
- Personalize the birthday card; have it signed by all the employees of your studio and most definitely write your name and a short message/birthday wish on the card.

- Have birthday cards printed with your studio name and/or an image of your yoga studio. The birthday girl/boy will immediately recognize your studio and there is a possibility that your card (your studio) will be hung on the wall during a certain period of time, for all of the visitors to notice.

- The card can be a combination of birthday wishes and a promotion. A card will give you the possibility to communicate a short message to the birthday girl/boy. Another idea is to add a birthday promotion: the student can follow a free yoga class on presentation of the birthday card. Again, a small effort for you that could mean a world of difference for your students. Moreover, this free class might just be the trigger to return to yoga or your studio.

New Year's Card
In line with the birthday card, you can also send a New Year's card with your wishes for the New Year. Again: make this card as personal as possible. A big studio might have to send pre-printed cards because it would take too much time to personally write and send all the cards. For a small studio, it is an extra opportunity to emphasize your personal approach and to personally thank your students for their presence during your classes. It ultimately is because of your students that you are able to do what you love most: teaching yoga classes in your own studio. Students will love to receive a card from you in which you thank them and wish them all the best for the New Year. As long as the message comes from your heart and is authentic, you will reach the students (their hearts) not only "on the mat" but also "off the mat".

Gift card
Gift cards make an original present for avid yogi(ni)s. It is also an original idea for students to give people in their environment the opportunity to get acquainted with yoga in an accessible way. Offering gift cards (online on your website or

webshop, or offline in your studio) is a way to attract students and earn some extra money.

Above "offline" activities can be used as an inspiration to make your studio grow and/or bring to the attention of your target audience. This list is certainly not exhausted, but I have tried to share ideas that are practical and easily accessible (as both time and money are concerned).

Did you carry out a successful promotional activity that hasn't been discussed in this book and would you like to share this with other yoga studio owners? Please email me at mathieu.van.steenberge@gmail.com. I might update this book with your experience or send your tip(s) to people who have subscribed to my newsletter.

7.5. Your studio as a marketing channel to spread your message

Besides the Internet, the analog or offline world, you also have your yoga studio (as part of the offline world) to attract students and to spread your message. The marketing activities as described above, are also part of the marketing that you do in your yoga studio. You could for instance put up a poster announcing a workshop or distribute flyers that allow your students' friends to join their yoga class for free. In addition to these activities, you have activities that are focused on attracting people in the vicinity of your studio (the incidental passer-by, for instance).

Next, I will discuss some marketing tools used to activate existing as well as new customers (to come more often, to follow a workshop, to spend more money during their visit to your yoga studio)

Sidewalk Signs

A sidewalk sign is an ideal way to attract the attention of passers-by. Your studio is by definition a local business that lives off people from the neighbourhood. It is therefore important that people who live near your studio, or regularly pass by your studio, know what you have to offer or what you can do for them. A sidewalk sign lowers the threshold to come inside and it also informs the incidental passer-by of your services. Would you stop out of curiosity to have a look at a downward facing dog sidewalk sign?

(source: https://www.instagram.com/p/LtXdo2NAkZ/)

Wall Signs

The facade of a business without advertising is like a pub without beer. Your facade is the spot to let your name (brand) be known and let the world know that you exist. Wall signs come in a variety of shapes, colors and sizes. You can choose lighted signs, a banner or a blade sign. You can also decide to only use your name, your logo or a combination of both as a wall sign. The most important thing to remember is that your wall sign is not placed too high and stands out (even at night).

Info meeting

Whereas a workshop (see below) is focused on "doing", the goal of an info meeting is more to introduce people in an informal and non-committal way (they don't have to pay) to yoga, you and your studio. It is also a time to ask questions, to eliminate prejudice and to remove any hurdles preventing people to begin doing yoga. Next to that, it is an opportunity to stimulate the people who are present at such an info meeting, to register for a beginner workshop.

Beginner workshops/series
Workshops aimed at attracting new students with little or no yoga experience are a great way to allow beginners to get acquainted with yoga, your way of teaching, your studio and your expertise. In order to attract new students to participate in your beginner workshop(s), you need to communicate your message through different channels. You can use an info evening, flyers, posters, your newsletter, your website/blog or you can ask your current customer database to invite their friends, acquaintance or family to participate in a beginner workshop in your studio.

To go one step further is to organize a series of beginner workshops/classes requiring the student to follow an x amount of classes for a certain amount of money. This way, you will increase the commitment of the beginning student (chances are that many beginners give up after only 1 class or workshop) and you will also generate more revenue by offering a beginner's yoga package.

After the workshop(s) it is important to follow-up in order to get the best result possible (which is to get the new students to stay).

Marketing activities to do after a beginner workshop:

1. Sending a follow-up email
At the start of the workshop you will have the students fill out a student information sheet with e.g. name, address, date of birth, sex and email address (tip: have each student fill out an information sheet, because this information is useful when sending a personal birthday card and/or New Year's card or sending newsletters). After the (series of) workshop(s), you can email your beginner students, asking for feedback (this feedback can help you get more insight into your way of teaching, the atmosphere of your studio, etc.). Next to that, you could use this email to launch a campaign, allowing the students to follow an x amount of classes for a certain amount of money. This way, you will motivate these beginning and

maybe hesitant students to continue their yoga practice. You are giving them a financial incentive to continue doing yoga.

2. Sending a thank you, birthday and/or New Year's card
Your goal is to (re)activate this beginners group and to also see them again after the workshop. It is therefore important to build top-of-mind awareness. By sending a personal card or email (possibly combining it with a promotional activity) you will ensure that yoga (and your studio) get back on the radar and make it easier to come in for another yoga class. Again, a little push in the right direction often proves to be enough for a beginner to return to yoga.

3. Organizing a follow-up workshop for beginners
Think of it as a child learning how to swim; first you go paddling in the pool together, then you take the child by the hand to go into deeper water and eventually, you let go. It is the same with yoga. The beginner workshop is like going paddling in shallow waters together, but afterwards students might feel like they have been let go in much deeper waters. Why not take an intermediate step? Design a follow-up workshop where you emphasize the alignment of the most common asanas, dive deeper into Patanjali's philosophy or where you introduce them to different styles of yoga and yoga teachers.

Workshops are a very powerful and efficient way to attract and retain more students but also to generate more income. A workshop is not an end goal, but the beginning of a - hopefully - long student-teacher relationship. Every relationship needs to be nourished, that is why a follow-up is crucial in successfully building the relationship.

Atmosphere in your studio
Burning candles, carefully adjusted lighting, a burning incense stick, the evaporation of essential oils, the cleanliness of the toilets, the temperature of the classroom, the privacy in changing rooms, the presence or absence of music, the way you teach or use your voice... these factors all contribute to

the atmosphere of your studio. There is only 1 advice: follow your heart!

Do you wish to gain more insight into the intangible atmosphere of your studio? You might want to consider surveying your students at regular intervals. You can send your students an email asking if they would like to give feedback (anonymously and without obligation) on their experience with your studio. You can design a short survey in which you ask your students about the things that are intangible.

Examples of such questions are:
- On a scale of 1 to 10, where 1 is not at all satisfied and 10 is very satisfied, how satisfied are you with the atmosphere of the studio?
- On a scale of 1 to 10, where 1 is not at all satisfied and 10 is very satisfied, how satisfied are you with the lighting in the studio?
- On a scale of 1 to 10, where 1 is not at all satisfied and 10 is very satisfied, how satisfied are you with the cleanliness of the studio?
- On a scale of 1 to 10, where 1 is not at all satisfied and 10 is very satisfied, how satisfied are you with the facilities for getting changed?
- On a scale of 1 to 10, where 1 is not at all satisfied and 10 is very satisfied, how satisfied are you with the way I teach?

It might be useful to ask open questions in addition to scoring questions and thus give your students the possibility to personally send in their opinion, suggestions or comments.

Online (free) tools that you can use to survey your customers:
- https://www.kwiksurveys.com
- https://www.surveygizmo.com
- https://www.surveymonkey.com
- https://freeonlinesurveys.com

7.6. Personal branding

"Regardless of age, regardless of position, regardless of the business we happen to be in, all of us need to understand the importance of branding. We are CEOs of our own companies: Me Inc. To be in business today, our most important job is to be head marketer for the brand called You." – **Tom Peters**

In Chapter 7.1, we touched upon the subject of branding. In this chapter I would like to investigate how we can develop ourselves as a brand. Without having to do research, I can tell you that in addition to easy accessibility, the price and your offer, the most important reason for visiting your studio is **YOU**. Just like the name, the logo and the interior leave a mark on your yoga studio, YOU leave an even bigger mark. As pointed out in chapter 7.1: everything can be copied, except for your own personal, authentic approach. It is consequently important to invest in this approach.

"Personal branding is the process of developing a "mark" that is created around your personal name or your career. You use this "mark" to express and communicate your skills, personality and values. The end goal is that the personal brand that you develop will build your reputation and help you to grow your network in a way that interests others. They will then seek you out for your knowledge and expertise." – **marketing.about.com**

This definition well summarizes what personal branding is. Below steps can help you in developing your personal brand.

❑ **Distinguishing yourself from other yoga teachers**
Your skills, your expertise, your personality, your values, your teaching style, the way you dress, the workshops you teach, the drinks you drink, the festival at which you are present, how you communicate with your students: it all contributes to the brand which is "YOU". They are all things that set you apart from other yoga teachers as well. Setting yourself apart is, however, not enough if you want to create your own personal brand.

❏ **Letting people know what you stand for**

In order to let people know what you stand for, you first have to figure out what it is you want to stand for. What do you do that you are most proud of? What do you do that is remarkable, measurable, evident, or distinctive? What have you accomplished that you can shamelessly brag about? If you want to build a personal brand, then you have to be focused on the activities that are of added value to your environment, that you can be proud of and, most importantly, that you can pat yourself on the back for. Lastly, you need to ask yourself what it is you want to be "famous" or known for? If you have the answers to all of these questions, then you are able to purposefully work on your personal brand.

❏ **Building a positive reputation**

Your reputation, qualities that are spontaneously linked to you and thereby your name, is the ultimate goal of personal branding. Everything you do, say and what you stand for, contribute to this reputation. Carefully select your words, actions and personal traits, but keep in mind that they suit your authentic self.

Do you want people to get to know you, talk about you and appreciate you for your positive traits or for your expertise about a certain subject? Then explore the following examples of how to make yourself interesting for others, how you can add value, increase your network and – last but not least – how you can do yourself proud.

1. Become an expert and/or authority

If you want others to look at you and consider you an authority, you of course need to have something significant to say. Invest in your knowledge. Being an expert in your field will definitely help you get recognition.

2. Create an online presence

Nowadays, having your own Facebook page and website is a minimum requirement to promote yourself online and build your personal brand.

You don't have one but you do have the ambition to promote

yourself? Waste no more time and create one right now (see chapter 7.3)! If you like to take it a step further, you could also become active on Twitter, Pinterest, Instagram, and a ton of other social media websites. Do what feel right and don't blindly follow what is written here. Listen to your heart, use your common sense/brains and when it feels right, take action.

3. Share!

If you have knowledge and/or skills that not everybody possesses, why keep it to yourself? Just like I am sharing my knowledge of marketing with you through this book, you could consider sharing your knowledge and skills with your target audience.

a. Music

Do you make music and like to entertain and inspire people with mantras, your own music or original covers? Invest some time in introducing people to your music. This could take place before or after class, during a workshop or spontaneously. Don't keep your music to yourself, but share it with your community and your target audience. Services such as Spotify, Mixcloud, Soundcloud, etc. make it very easy to share your music with your target audience.

b. Movies

Do you have tips & tricks about asanas? Do you want to share your experiences? Make a short movie and share it on YouTube, your website, your Facebook page, your newsletter… Why not upload complete yoga classes to YouTube?

c. Articles

Do you have good writing skills? Share your knowledge and experience on your blog or write articles for a yoga magazine.

d. Content

Did you find an interesting and relevant article, movie,

event, or workshop? Share it before, after or during class with your students or on your Facebook page or website. You get my drift!

4. Send out press releases

In Chapter 7.1, I introduced you to the possibilities that a press release can offer. Next to sharing interesting, relevant and original information with the media, the press release also offers the opportunity to get your name out there.

5. Look for opportunities to address your target audience

Keep an eye out for opportunities to share your knowledge and skills with others. You could teach a yoga class at a local festival or you could have an info meeting at the local sports club, speaking about the benefits of yoga for athletes. And how about giving lectures to students that want to become physical education teachers, dietitian or something else that might complement yoga? How about teaching yoga to dance students every week? Get out there, talk to people and share your love for yoga!

6. Work on your personal teaching style

Even good yoga teachers can always become better. Keep investing in perfecting your teaching style, your knowledge, your tone of voice, and the support and alignment of students. Learn, evolve and share with those around you.

Because personal brand is personal, it is impossible to list all of the ways to promote yourself and make a strong personal brand. In this book, I will describe some of the basic steps that you can take in order to market yourself.

Start at the beginning, follow your heart and continue to be authentic. You cannot fake a personal brand, because the truth will come out sooner or later. Your network of friends, colleagues, students and customers is the most important marketing channel you have at your disposal. What they say about you and your contribution is invaluable when it comes to building a good reputation and a strong personal brand. The key is to find ways to continue to nourish, stimulate and inspire your network. The ultimate goal of personal branding is that your name is accepted as an authority and that people are talking about you (word-of-mouth).

Do you want to know more personal branding and how to promote yourself? Definitely check the following online articles:

- ❏ "How to Create Your Personal Brand in 6 Easy Steps" https://www.pickthebrain.com/blog/how-to-create-your-personal-brand-in-6-easy-steps
- ❏ "The Brand Called You" https://www.fastcompany.com/28905/brand-called-you
- ❏ "The First Step To Building Your Personal Brand https://www.forbes.com/sites/dailymuse/2012/02/14/the-first-step-to-building-your-personal-brand/
- ❏ "Personal Branding 101" https://www.forbes.com/sites/lisaquast/2013/04/22/personal-branding-101/
- ❏ "How to Brand Yourself" https://brandyourself.com/info/seo/how_to_brand_yourself

Do you like reading more books and want to know more about the art of personal branding? Definitely read the following books:
- ❏ "Branding pays: The Five-Step System to Reinvent Your Personal Brand" – by Karen Kang
- ❏ "Personal Branding For Dummies"– by Susan Chritton

7.7. Partnerships
A good place to start looking for new customers is a place where people already spend money on a product or service that is similar to yours.

2 important reasons for considering this are:
1. These people demonstrate that they might be interested in your offer.

2. These people demonstrate that they have the money and are willing to spend on products or services that are similar to yours.

Expand your network and introduce yourself to every party that offers a complementary service or product, similar to yours. I spontaneously think of:
- Massage parlors
- Dietitians
- Chiropractors
- Osteopaths
- Physical therapists
- Manual therapists
- Doctors
- Organic shops
- Ecology shops (e.g. eco clothing shop)
- Running-, swimming-, dance- and sports clubs
- Fitness centers

7.8. Customer satisfaction as a basis for word-of-mouth
It has been mentioned often in this book: your students, your customers, are the reason of your existence. Not only do they generate the necessary income in the short term, in the long term they are partly responsible for the success of your studio. If they are satisfied, chances are that they will share this positive feeling about you, your studio and your employees with their friends and acquaintances. This word-of-mouth advertising is still the most powerful and effective form of marketing. That's why I feel that customer service is marketing and marketing is customer service. In everything you do, your focus has to be on the customer and you should ask yourself how your customer would experience this. Common sense and some empathy go a long way! All your activities should be aimed at making your students (more) happy. If you touch their hearts, you will reap long-term benefits. This means that you will have to occasionally sow the seeds before reaping the harvest or that you sow because you like doing so, without expecting to reap a good harvest. Doing (business) from your

heart, will touch the hearts of your students anyway.

It goes without saying that we keep the ROI (Return On Investment) in mind when having a sales promotion, meaning that your input should be measured against your output. Many students would be very satisfied if all your classes would be for free. Such an offer however wouldn't be realistic as you would soon be without income. In short: use your common sense and remember that customer service doesn't revolve around free giveaways. A friendly smile and a floor free of dust and hair could have more effect than a free class. To make customer satisfaction more tangible, you could casually ask your students if they are satisfied with your studio and your classes. This is not only time consuming, but will also compel your students to answer positively, as not all students feel comfortable sharing their unsalted opinion with you. A (online and anonymous) customer satisfaction research is the tool of choice to measure customer satisfaction.

Customer satisfaction research
Try to compose a list of the factors that influence your satisfaction with a yoga teacher and/or studio. Evaluate yourself and/or your studio on these points by giving a score between 1 and 10 where 1 is very unsatisfied and 10 is very satisfied. Lastly, you need to ask yourself whether or not you would recommend your studio to others. This question gives you immediate insight into the customer satisfaction and therefore the growth potential of your studio.
(source: https://www.checkmarket.com/blog/ net-promoter-score/)

Depending on the scores your students give, you are able to divide your students into 3 groups:
1. Promoters: students giving a score of 9 or 10
2. Passives: students giving a score of 7 or 8
3. Detractors: students giving a score lower or equal to 6

The three groups combined are 100%. The Net Promoter Score (NPS) is a score indicating how well your studio does in terms of customer satisfaction. In order to calculate the NPS, we have to subtract the percentage of Detractors from the percentage of Promoters. If the NPS is bigger than 0, the result is positive. If the NPS is smaller than 0, you have very unsatisfied customers and there is a strong possibility they will drop out.

Your goal is to have as many Promoters among your students as possible. They are the ones who promote your studio to their friends, family and acquaintances. The Passives are a very interesting group, as they are not a 100% satisfied with your approach and therefore linger between the Detractors and Promoters.

If they remain unfulfilled, they will join the Detractors. The Detractors are a group of students that are likely to drop out and go to another studio. It is wise to include an open question in your research for both the Passives and the Detractors, asking them about possible improvements. The answers to this open question will allow you to get insight into the individual needs and expectations of your students. Some of these answers prove to be so valuable that you may want to take them up immediately. You can also expect unjustified feedback expressed by only 1 student. It is up to you whether or not to ignore this feedback. It is unrealistic to have 100% satisfied customers, but it should always be your goal to strive for 100% customer satisfaction.

If you have employees in your studio, it is wise to involve them in your customer approach. This may involve training your employees in welcoming students to making them aware that a tidy room has an influence on the satisfaction of your students. Customer satisfaction is a team effort!

Handling complaints
When people give a comment or negative feedback, our initial response is to immediately get defensive. Tip: don't immediately go on the defensive, but embrace this feedback. Even if you don't agree with the feedback, it is still valuable to

you, because it is the perception of one of your students. You can later decide what you will or won't do with the feedback that you received.

If you receive verbal feedback or comments, apply the LSC-principle:
> Listening:
  Be open to feedback and actively listen to the person who shares his or her feedback with you.
> Summarizing:
  Summarize – after your student has shared his/her opinion with you– out loud to make sure that you're talking about the same thing.
> Clarification:
  Ask additional questions to fully grasp what has been said.

By using the LSC-principle, you will first shut off all your emotions and focus on the person sharing the comment with you. This also allows you to get a clearer image of the complaint by summarizing what the student is saying and possibly by asking additional questions in case it is not yet a 100% clear.

Sometimes, it is good to clarify the context or to give more insight into the how and why of your actions. Avoid discussions with students –even if you are right- because you will always lose. After all, the customer is king (which is not to say that you have to let them walk all over you).

Customer Complaint Iceberg
Everybody knows the story of the Titanic where the small iceberg as seen from a distance, turns out to be a giant iceberg below the water surface.

The same goes for complaints. We often only get to see the tip of the iceberg. Many customers don't take the effort to complain, but instead go to the competition, which makes it that much more important to pay attention to the customer that does take the time to share a complaint with you. The one complaint might just be the tip of the iceberg? An anonymous (online) customer satisfaction research can allow you to explore this iceberg.

Service recovery paradox
Ironically, handling a complaint leads to greater customer satisfaction, provided that the complaint is handled and resolved adequately. A complaint thus offers the opportunity to strengthen the relationship with your student.

Because customer satisfaction and word-of-mouth are of crucial importance for the growth of your yoga studio, I recommend taking these following book recommendations to heart. These books are a source of inspiration to better serve and longer keep your customers:

- ❏ "Exceptional Service, Exceptional Profit" – by Leonardo Inghilleri
- ❏ "Secret Service" – by John R. Dijulius
- ❏ "Fish!" – by Stephen C. Lundin
- ❏ "Raving fans" – by Kenneth Blanchard

7.9. To better serve and longer keep existing customers
We know that making and keeping customers satisfied is our absolute goal if we want to succeed. The better you know your customers, the closer the relationship is, and the better you can tailor your services and approach to your customer's needs. The relationship with your customer is the key to having a successful yoga studio.

If we take a closer look at the relationship with your customers, then a few questions arise:

- How can we get to know our students better and therefore serve our students better?
- Where can we store the acquired (personal) knowledge about our students?

- How do we retrieve this information when needed?
- How can we solidify the relationship with our students?
- How can we reactivate students to start practicing yoga again?
- How do we get loyal students?

I will try to give practically useful answers to each of the above questions.

Customer Relationship Management (CRM)

"Customer Relationship Management (CRM) - the overall process of building and maintaining profitable customer relationships by delivering superior customer value and satisfaction." – Dr Philip Kotler

How is it done?

Interrogating your students isn't an option for obtaining personal information that helps you to optimalize your services.

You could ask each (new) student who enters the studio to fill out a student information sheet. In many gyms or clubs this is common practice and students will fill out an information sheet with pleasure.

We need to ask ourselves two things:
1. What do we want to know about our students?
2. Why do we want to know this?

The answer to both questions has to be that we want to gather information that helps us better cater for the individual needs of students so that they will have an even better experience.

Below questions can serve as an inspiration for creating your student information sheet:

- Name (people like to be addressed by their first name)
- Gender (gives you insight into the male to female ratio

in your studio)

- Date of birth (so you can surprise them on their birthday. It also gives you insight into your target market)
- Address (you can send a card wishing them a happy birthday or a happy New Year)
- Email (you can inform them about workshops, teaching schedules)
- Ask if they want to subscribe to your newsletter
- Ask about possible (chronic) pain and/or injuries
- Ask for the reason why they do yoga (you will be amazed at the reasons that people will give)
- Ask how they learned about you or your studio (you will get an insight into which channels are important in your marketing strategy)
- Ask if they have any hobbies other than yoga (this information allows you to offer tailor-made workshops)

Now that you have all of the relevant information for each of your students, it is important that you save this data so as to be able to access it at a later time. You can save the information in Excel, but if you want to relieve yourself of your administrative tasks, focus more on teaching and the smooth running of your studio, then I recommend purchasing a Customer Relationship Management System.

A Customer Relationship Management System or CRM-system offers plenty advantages:

1. It is relatively cheap if you calculate how much time you spend today on keeping your client data up-to-date.
2. It is easy to set up seeing as most popular CRM-systems can be found online and you don't have to install anything.
3. Most systems work seamlessly with other systems (like the software you use for your newsletter).
4. In addition to a Customer Relationship Management System, you also have a Point of Sale (POS) System

that allows you to identify revenues for a particular class, day, week, month, or year.

5. You can activate online bookings for classes and/or workshops so that people can register and pay entirely online. You will no longer lose time on the follow-up of registrations, payments, refunds, counting the number of registrations...

6. Days after their first class, new students are able to receive an automated, but personalized email in which you welcome them to your studio or suggest a particular workshop or class.

7. Most systems are equipped with a planning module that allows you to easily schedule your employees' classes and calculate how much you have to pay them.

8. How would you feel about people who registered for a workshop automatically receiving a text message or email reminder?

9. Some systems allow you to generate gift certificates that you can then sell in your studio or on your website.

10. You can completely digitalize your studio by purchasing a corresponding EPOS-system. With an EPOS-system, you can replace your paper membership cards, punch cards, subscriptions, and gift certificates by a digital card. With a card reader, you are able to read a student card and process all the information digitally.

A CRM-system gives you the opportunity to get more insight into your clients:

1. Which students spend the most money in your studio?
This information allows you to subdivide your students based on the money they spend in your studio. This information is important to know when they 'suddenly' drop out. A student who spends $50 per month in your studio has a greater impact on the financial growth of your studio than a student who spends $10 per month. It is also interesting to know which students spend $10 per month so you design a marketing campaign to get these students to maybe spend $50 a month as well.

2. Which students drop out after a certain number of classes, weeks or months?

This information allows you to further build on the knowledge you've gained in the above-mentioned point. If you have a student who comes to practice yoga in your studio 3 times a week on average and 'suddenly' doesn't show up, then it is good to find out why that student stopped visiting your studio. A CRM-system allows you to filter those students who failed to show up after an x number of classes of an x number of weeks. You can design a campaign to get these dropouts to return to your studio. Such a campaign can comprise of sending an email in which you indicate that you have missed them in your classes, or in which you check to see if everything is (physically) alright or in which you offer a discount if they come to the studio this week.

3. Which age groups are represented in your studio?

In Chapter 4.1 we already spoke about analyzing and knowing your target audience. With a CRM-system you get an instant insight into which age groups are represented in your studio. This can serve as a basis for better serving the needs of the current audiences or for attracting new audiences.

4. What is the male to female ratio in your studio?

The age of your students is a part of your target audience analysis. The male to female ratio can also be used as a basis for attracting new target audiences of for better serving the current audiences.

5. Which (postal) areas are most strongly represented?

In Chapter 4.2 we spoke about yoga studios primarily being a local matter. The majority of your students will live close to your studio. By means of a CRM-system, you can visually map in which area, postal code or city your students live or come from. This information allows you to improve your direct marketing activities, for example in specific (postal) areas or neighborhoods.

On the Internet, there are dozens of CRM-systems (designed for yoga studios).

An overview of the most popular systems:
- ❑ https://www.mindbodyonline.com/yoga
- ❑ https://www.karmasoftonline.com/
- ❑ https://www.iclasspro.com/
- ❑ https://www.perfectmind.com/
- ❑ https://www.zenplanner.com/yoga-studio-software

Questions you definitely have to ask if you are planning on purchasing a CRM-system:

1. How long does the company exist and how many customers (yoga studios) use the system?
2. Is the software web-based of do you have to install software on your computer or server?
3. Does the system allow you to safely process payments (PCI compliant)?
4. Which features are important to you?
5. How much do you have to pay (per month)?

Now that we know how to get to know our students better, what role customer satisfaction plays, how to activate drop-out students and what a CRM-system can mean to your studio, I would like to give you more insight into the importance of repeat purchases and how we are able to encourage students to repeat purchase.

Customer loyalty and the impact on repeat purchases
In every company, not matter how big or small, the focus is on the customer (at least in theory). Experience shows us that many companies struggle with unhappy customers, customers who leave and go to a competitor. Having a customer-oriented approach is crucial if you wish to have a sound financial growth. These customers are the ones who provide the much-needed revenue that pays your rent, your loans, and your wages. It is therefore necessary to turn satisfied customers into loyal customers. Loyal customers are customers who

have an emotional connection with you or your studio and visit or recommend your studio more often because of it.

In order to turn satisfied customers into loyal customers, you can develop loyalty campaigns.

Benefits of loyalty campaigns:
1. Students feel appreciated. On almost every receipt you will find a "thank you for your purchase". It is one thing to print this on a receipt, but it's something completely different to genuinely thank your customers and make them feel special. A loyalty program or campaign can make your student feel special and appreciated.

2. A loyalty campaign encourages your customers to visit your studio again. When students have different options to choose from, a reward to visit your studio may be enough to influence their choice in selecting your studio. If your campaign has a time limit, you will encourage them to visit your studio sooner than they may have planned.

Below activities can increase customer loyalty:
1. Most important is to have a genuinely kind and correct attitude towards your students. Opening the door, a sincere and friendly smile, an informal chat...they all contribute to the satisfaction and loyalty of your students.

2. Remember the names of your students and use these. People like to be addressed by their first name. It increases the involvement of students and you make them feel special.

3. Avoid *win-lose* discussions. Your customers are always right, even if they're not. Some customers can get in your hair by wanting to have endless discussions. It is good to be assertive (make you arguments clear in a correct yet resolute way), but know that having endless

discussions will push the customers further away from you.

4. Students are able to pay in your studio for e.g. a single class, a 10-class punch card, or a monthly subscription. You could offer the students who pay for a single class a customer card that, after 10 classes/stamps, gets them 1 free class. It's also possible to have them select a random gift (which might contain a key chain or sweat band of your studio) after those 10 classes. This way, you will reward the students who don't visit your studio often and motivate them to continue to come at the same time (because they will miss out on their stamp and their reward otherwise)

5. Also reward your loyal customers. Reward does not mean to give something away for free. A birthday card or discount on a workshop might be an extra reason to continue visiting your studio.

6. Even though customers like to be rewarded, they also like giving to others. You could find a local charity and donate a certain amount of money after a certain number of visits to your studio. If you also make this campaign visible in your studio, you create a sense of involvement and community.

7. Find partners! You don't have to reward your students with your own products or services. There might be a beauty salon that is looking to find new customers. You may want to work together in rewarding the customers who have visited your studio an x amount of times with a free massage?

8. Explore what Perkville (https://www.perkville.com/) can offer your studio. Perkville is a service that allows local business to set up a loyalty program in only a couple of minutes. Perkville is free of charge for your students and offers monthly subscriptions to businesses. Make

sure to read the case study of how Charm City Yoga, a chain of 6 studios in Baltimore, saw its monthly revenues increase by rewarding loyal customers and reactivating customers who had been inactive for 30-60 days by automatic reminder emails. Perkville also works together with the CRM-system of MindBodyOnline (https://www.mindbodyonline.com/apps/perkville).

> ➤ "Case Study: Yoga Chain Ups Revenue With Perkville Loyalty Program"
> http://streetfightmag.com/2012/07/25/case-study-yoga-chain-increases-revenue-with-perkville-program/

Do you want to deepen your customer loyalty knowledge? Make sure to check the follow articles:
- ❑ "6 Ways to Build Customer Loyalty"
  https://www.entrepreneur.com/article/226064
- ❑ "Customer Loyalty: The Ultimate Guide"
  https://blog.hubspot.com/customer-success/customer-loyalty

Books that I recommend for getting more insight into customer loyalty and customer satisfaction:
- ❑ "Customer Satisfaction Is Worthless, Customer Loyalty Is Priceless" – by Jeffrey Gitomer
- ❑ "The Art of Membership" – by Sheri Jacobs
- ❑ "The Effortless Experience" – by Matthew Dixon

7.10. Generating extra revenue
In the previous chapters we have discussed:
- How to attract new students
- How to motivate existing students to come more often
- How to reactivate inactive students
- Which advantages a CRM-system has to offer
- What the importance of customer satisfaction and customer loyalty is

We do this so we can achieve the ultimate goal of running a financially healthy yoga studio. Unfortunately, it may not be enough to fill up your classes with students every day and to cover all the costs at the end of the month. In this chapter, I will elaborate on how we can also earn money with other activities, in addition to our core business (namely teaching and filling up classes with students). These activities are complementary to your yoga studio and yoga classes and can bring in the extra money that you need so that your dream in the long run, doesn't turn into a nightmare.

You are selling a positive experience to students by teaching a yoga class. Next to selling a yoga class, there are also other products, services or activities that are in line with what you're doing and that your students might be interested in. Your goal is not merely to make more money, but also to build a better relationship with your students by responding to their needs. You will optimize their overall experience in your studio, so that your students will always leave satisfied.

Activities you can offer are:
- ❑ **Opening a yoga shop:**
  I'm not talking about setting up a completely new store (although this could perfectly complement your current activity as a yoga studio owner). I am however talking about turning a forgotten corner of your studio or reception desk into a space where you can offer yoga articles for sale. In addition to such a retail corner in your studio, you could also consider starting a webshop.

  - o What can you sell in your studio or webshop?
    - ▪ *Yoga Essentials*
      Think of yoga mats, yoga mat bags, towels, blocks, bolsters, straps, blankets, eye pillows, and water bottles.

    - ▪ *Items with your name and logo*
      You can offer T-shirts, sweatbands,

postcards, pens, key chains, coffee or tea cups, water bottles with your name and logo. You don't have to immediately start selling all of these articles, but my advice to every studio is to at least sell T-shirts with your name and logo. Students who love your studio and take pride in what they do, will gladly buy your T-shirt. This doesn't only generate extra income, but you're also building a strong community of loyal visitors/fans who promote your studio.

- **Yoga wear**
  Offering your favorite clothing line for sale can be a beautiful addition to your yoga studio and will undoubtedly be welcomed by your students.

- **Books, CDs and movies**
  During our classes, we usually don't have enough time to feed our students with knowledge on yoga philosophy, anatomy, and mantras...Make sure to offer them a selection of your favorite books, CDs and movies, so that they can continue to learn at their own pace and in the comfort of their own home.

- **Make your own DVD**
  Why not make your own series of lessons, film it and burn it to a DVD so motivated students can buy your DVD and follow their favorite yoga class at home or on vacation?

- **Accessories**
  Salt lamps, incense, candles, oil evaporators, aromatherapy sprays,

chakra flags, posters, and Buddha statues...In short, all products that contribute to the atmosphere.

- **Eating, drinking and food supplements** (Ayurvedic) herbal supplements, YogiTea, Coconut water, energy bars...

It goes without saying that above list is not exhaustive. My advice is that you can sell anything, as long as it has a connection to yoga. Keep your supply limited and don't clutter your studio with stuff. Students may think you are losing focus on teaching, that you are desperate and in other words don't earn enough with your core activity, namely teaching.

It may seem that you would sell everything just to earn some extra money. This will erode trust that students have in you and your studio. In other words, stay away from things that have nothing to do with yoga and keep your focus on what you do best: teaching!

❑ Workshops

In addition to giving your regular classes, you can also give workshops to meet the needs of your students on the one hand and to generate income on the other hand. Workshops can match class themes and enable you to further explore the theme. A workshop also gives you the opportunity to attract new students or to stimulate the curiosity of inactive students. Organizing a workshop is also a good time to send your students a newsletter, to update your website or blog or to distribute flyers.

❏ **Teacher Trainings**
If you have the necessary experience, qualifications, and passion, then organizing teacher trainings for future yoga teachers might be something for you?

❏ **Retreats**
Why not go on a secluded retreat with a group of yoga enthusiasts for a couple of days, a weekend or a whole week? In addition to nurturing the commitment towards your students, a retreat also gives a sense of unity. This commitment and sense of unity lead to a closer connection with your students, which allows you to be more attuned to their (individual) needs.

❏ **Tap into a new target audience**
In addition to the classes that are being taught at your yoga studio, there are plenty of possibilities that allow you to further spread your passion. Below you will find several examples that might inspire you:

    o **Private classes (at home or in your studio)**
      Some people prefer the individual guidance to group classes and some are simply not able to free their schedule and attend your group classes. Private classes may well be a great solution for this target audience!

    o **Business Yoga**
      Business Yoga is booming. More and more companies invest in their "human capital" and recognize the importance of happy, healthy employees. Business Yoga can make a valuable contribution.

    o **Pregnancy Yoga**
      Pregnancy Yoga allows for a smoother labor and delivery by preparing the participants both physically and mentally. It also develops a bond between mother and child. The combination of

breathing exercises, yoga postures, meditation and relaxation teaches the future mothers to become more aware of the changes in their bodies as well as their lives.

- ○ *(After school) Children's Yoga*
  If you love children and want to practice yoga with them in a playful manner, children's yoga can be a beautiful addition to your current 'traditional' yoga classes.

- ○ **Organic juice bar**
  If you have the space and the time to sell smoothies or fresh juices after class, then the purchase of a juicer might be the thing for you. A fruit juicer allows you to quickly make delicious juices to offer to your students. It's a great way to conclude your yoga session and to socialize or network.

- ○ **Gift cards**
  Gift cards make an original present for avid yogi(ni)s. It is also an original idea for students to give people in their environment the opportunity to get acquainted with yoga in an accessible way. Offering gift cards (online on your website or webshop, or offline in your studio) is a way to attract students and earn extra money.

- ○ **Calendar**
  For each month, you can choose a student or a teacher performing his or her favorite asana. Such a calendar will make a fantastic promotional gift or an opportunity to organize an end-of-year activity. It could also be an opportunity to earn some extra money, in addition to your yoga classes. You can sell the calendar in your studio, on your website or during workshops. You may want to donate the

proceeds to a (local) charity? What better way is there to start the New Year?

Epilogue

It goes without saying that there are other possibilities to promote your studio and/or yourself.

Your experience and feedback are therefore very important to me. If you have a positive experience with something that hasn't been discussed in this book, I encourage you to share this with me. You can contact me with your experiences (mathieuvansteenberge@gmail.com or https://www.facebook.com/mathieu.van.steenberge). I might update this book with your experience or send your tip(s) to the people who have subscribed to my newsletter. Sharing is caring, remember: ;-)

My passion to help people is what made me write this book. I hope from the bottom of my heart that I've managed to teach you something about marketing and how you can use marketing for your yoga studio. I have greatly enjoyed the writing process and - as with many things in life - the journey is sometimes more important than the final destination.

Did you enjoy this book? Do you wish to share something with me? Or just say hello?
Send an email to mathieu.van.steenberge@gmail.com or connect with me on Facebook:
https://www.facebook.com/mathieu.van.steenberge.

May the sun light your path!

Namaste,
Mathieu

Feel free to connect with me:
www.facebook.com/mathieuvansteenberge
www.instagram.com/mathieuvansteenberge